Walking with
GERARD MANLEY
HOPKINS

Also by Robert Waldron
published by Paulist Press

Walking with Thomas Merton
Walking with Henri Nouwen
Walking with Kathleen Norris
Thomas Merton: Master of Attention
The Wounded Heart of Thomas Merton

Walking with
GERARD MANLEY HOPKINS

A Poet's Journey

Robert Waldron

Paulist Press
New York / Mahwah, NJ

Quotes from Gerard Manley Hopkins' poetry are taken from *The Poems of Gerard Manley Hopkins*, ed. W. H. Gardner and N. H. Mackenzie (London: Oxford University Press, 1967), and from Gerard Manley Hopkins, ed. Catherine Phillips, The Oxford Authors (Oxford and New York: Oxford University Press, 1986).

Cover design by Sharyn Banks
Book design by Lynn Else

Library of Congress Cataloging-in-Publication Data

Waldron, Robert G.
    Walking with Gerard Manley Hopkins : a poet's journey / Robert Waldron.
        p. cm.
    Includes bibliographical references (p.   ).
    ISBN 978-0-8091-4739-7 (alk. paper)
    1. Hopkins, Gerard Manley, 1844—1889. 2. Hopkins, Gerard Manley, 1844—1889—Religion. 3. Christian poetry, English—19th century—History and criticism. 4. Experience (Religion) in literature. 5. Spirituality in literature. 6. Poets, English—19th century—Biography. 7. Jesuits—England—Biography. I. Title.
    PR4803.H44Z916 2011
    821'.8—dc22

                                                                2011018678

Published by Paulist Press
997 Macarthur Boulevard
Mahwah, New Jersey 07430

www.paulistpress.com

Printed and bound in the
United States of America

Contents

Preface

Gerard Manley Hopkins was a celibate, and he remained faithful to this state of life to the end of his life; but living in Dublin as a professor at University College, he was removed from all those who loved him, his large family and his best friends. He lived among the Irish, most of whom loathed the English. He was literally a stranger in a strange land: "To seem the stranger lies my lot, my life / Among strangers."

Hopkins was also "strange" in another fashion, one he cannot overtly write about in his poems, journals, or letters: he was likely a homosexual man. All of the major biographers and critics of Hopkins have commented at length on this aspect of his life, the great secret of his life. It must have been a constant drain of energy to maintain his guard, to control his eyes, to make certain that what he looked upon did not betray him. He well understood the danger of mortal beauty: "To what serves mortal beauty—dangerous." He had always to master his gaze lest it lead him down perilous paths of sexual longing. It is no wonder that his preferred ascetic practice was the "custody of eyes."

Hopkins' every action was dedicated to Christ. His prayers, his practice of custody of the eyes, his denial of food and other pleasures were done to please his Beloved. And yet in Dublin he fell into a slough of despair, which nearly swallowed him completely. Why? Perhaps being so exquisitely and sensitively human, he needed to be touched. In *Hamlet*, Shakespeare says, "Readiness is all." In *King Lear*, he says, "Ripeness is all." Our modern poet Anne Sexton, in her book *An Awful Rowing toward God*, says, "Touch is all." Human beings need to touch and to be touched. Scientific studies have shown that prematurely born babies if not touched quickly die; those who are caressed thrive.

The lack of touch must have exerted a tremendous toll on Hopkins, a man so vibrantly alive, so acutely aware of the world around him, so attracted to people. When he was young, he had scores of friends, some of whom he fell in love with, as he did with Digby Dolben, whom he met once, a heart-rending echo of Dante's once-in-a-lifetime transforming glance of Beatrice.

We must, therefore, understand this aspect of Hopkins' life in order to comprehend his "Terrible Sonnets." It is my contention that Hopkins suffered much from shame. His sonnets reveal that he had led a blameless life, devoting it to *imitatio Christi*. And by all accounts, Hopkins was a saintly man although it is unlikely that he ever considered himself saintly. But such knowledge does not nullify the possibility that he likely felt shame, for I firmly believe that he *knew* he was a homosexual man, although that very term did not exist when he lived. He was surely aware, however, of the time-worn expression: "the love that dare not speak its name."

Across the Atlantic Ocean, another poet, also a homosexual man, felt no shame nor guilt for being attracted to other men. He was raised a Quaker and was a good, religious Christian himself, but he was a man comfortable within his own skin. Hopkins had read his verse; he writes:

> I always knew in my heart Walt Whitman's mind to be more like my own than any other man living. As he is a very great scoundrel this is not a pleasant confession.

And this also makes me the more desirous to read him
and the more determined that I will not.

About Hopkins' comment, American critic Harold Bloom later
says, "Hopkins, I suspect, read more widely in Whitman than he
cared to admit."*

Hopkins had certainly detected Whitman's homosexuality, and he
was attracted to him because he saw himself in Whitman; consequently, he denied himself the pleasure of knowing this kindred spirit
also by the ascetic "custody of the eyes"—by sacrificing his desire to
read him.

When you come to the section of this book addressing the Terrible
Sonnets, keep in mind that there is a distinct *possibility* that Hopkins'
repressed sexuality may have contributed to the anguish of the midlife
crisis he endured in Dublin while teaching at University College.

* Harold Bloom, *Walt Whitman*. Bloom's Modern Critical Views
(New York: Chelsea House, 2006), 229—30.

A Note on the Poetry Texts

The poems of Gerard Manley Hopkins from which verses are quoted in this book can be found in full in the following editions:

Gerard Manley Hopkins, ed. Catherine Phillips. The Oxford Authors. Oxford and New York: Oxford University Press, 1986.

The Poems of Gerard Manley Hopkins, ed. W. H. Gardner and N. H. Mackenzie. London: Oxford University Press, 1967.

Introduction

Gerard Manley Hopkins (1844—89) was born into an upper-middle-class family in Stratford, England, the eldest of eight children. He and his family were devoted members of the High Anglican Church, a religion that the young Hopkins found to be attractive, convincing, holy, and beautiful. His father owned a successful marine insurance company, which allowed the family to move to the fashionable suburb of Oak Hill in Hampstead, outside London. There Hopkins could climb trees, a favorite pastime, from which he had a clear view of London in the distance.

Between the ages of eight and sixteen Hopkins was a pupil at Highgate School, whose headmaster, Oxford-graduate Reverend John Bradley Dyne, was infamous for flogging "unruly" boys with a birch. Highgate was one of many grammar schools flourishing in England at this time. Although it was not as prestigious as Eton or Harrow, Hopkins received a fine education there; in fact, he excelled academically, winning all the coveted prizes in English verse, Latin prose, and classical history. His weaknesses, mathematics and hand-writing, kept him a few times from becoming the top of his class, but did not interfere with his winning an exhibition (scholarship) in 1862 to Oxford University's Balliol College.

Hopkins attended Oxford at a time when some of England's greatest intellectual luminaries were still present: the poet Matthew Arnold (1822—88); the novelist (also Hopkins' Oxford tutor) Walter Pater (1839—94); and Edward Pusey (1800—82), one of the founders of the Tractarian Movement (named after religious tracts written by its followers and later to be called the Oxford Movement). The Tractarians were a group of Anglican churchmen attempting to redefine the relationship of the Church of England to the Roman Catholic Church; the last of the tracts brought Anglicanism close to Roman Catholicism by encouraging the return of many Catholic rituals discarded during the Dissolution, rituals considered too Catholic by the bishop of Oxford, who tried unsuccessfully to suppress the Tractarian series.

The greatest influence on Hopkins was John Henry Newman (1801—90), the leader of the Oxford Movement. Although he was no longer a teacher or Anglican priest at Oxford when Hopkins arrived, his presence still lingered there and still influenced gifted intellectuals such as Hopkins.

Before he even arrived at Oxford, Hopkins had begun to doubt the legitimacy of Anglican priesthood. He also believed in the Catholic teaching of the Real Presence, considering it the true foundation of Christian faith; without it, he observed, religion is dangerously somber and lacks logic. In fact, he went so far as to say that if he were ever to doubt the Real Presence, he would instantly become an atheist.

Hopkins was greatly influenced by Newman's autobiography, *Apologia Pro Vita Sua.* Newman published the *Apologia* in 1864 in response to the written attack on his integrity by Charles Kingsley (1819—75), the well-known Anglican clergyman and author of the novel *Westward Ho!* The gist of Kingsley's claim was that Newman had pretended to be an Anglican when in fact he was "popish," a derogatory term for Catholic; Kingsley assailed Newman for not being honest and truthful with his large following at Oxford. To set the record straight about his conversion to Catholicism and thereby refute Kingsley's attack, Newman composed his autobiography, a masterful counterattack that won for him much praise and sympathy from the people of England, not only for his apologetics but also for his elegant prose style. Newman also had another reason to write his autobiography: he intended it to bring more people, particularly brilliant men like Hopkins, into the Catholic Church. Having already begun to question the validity of the Church of England and after reading Newman, Hopkins decided to be received into the Catholic Church. Newman himself accepted him into the Church in 1866.

As with most young men, Hopkins was undecided about his vocation. He had thought he might become a painter but feared that such a profession was dangerous to the passions. Hopkins was always comfortable with drawing nature according to the critic John Ruskin's manual of drawing, which stressed acute attention to nature's details. But an artist must also be trained to draw the human body, and Hopkins was anxious about this, as is revealed in the first line of his poem "To What Serves Mortal Beauty?": "To what serves mortal beauty—dangerous; does set dancing blood"; thus, he renounced the idea because he felt *too* attracted to physical beauty, which might arouse the passions and lead to sin. (Two of Hopkins' brothers, it should be mentioned, became successful painters and illustrators.)

The new convert tried teaching at the Oratory School, an outreach of the Birmingham Oratory founded by Newman, who, with his closest followers, had become members of the religious congregation founded in the sixteenth century by St. Philip Neri—"Oratorians." Newman had established the Oratory School to educate the male children of the gentry, providing a traditional English public school education along with an emphasis on Catholic teaching. Hopkins daily taught five boys of the fifth form and two advanced private pupils after dinner every day except Saturday. He was not attracted to educating youngsters and found the work physically tiring (his health was always frail), but he was fond of his students and called them his children.

Hopkins did feel drawn to a religious vocation, however, and he discussed with Newman which religious order he should join. Newman remained neutral, allowing the young man to choose for himself. In fact, he discouraged Hopkins from making a hasty decision about religious life, but Hopkins disregarded Newman's advice. At the time, Hopkins was attracted to the Benedictines and the Jesuits; he finally chose the severe, rigorous Jesuits, entering their order as a novice in 1868.

Up to this time, Hopkins had been composing poetry. He indeed had the right to be called a poet even though he had not published a volume of verse. Like Emily Dickinson, he remained unknown as a poet during his lifetime. On entering the Jesuits, he burned his poetry in what he describes in a very brief journal entry for May 11, 1868, as his "Slaughter of the Innocents." Hopkins felt that writing was a worldly indulgence incompatible with his new life as a Catholic convert, and that his major concern should be matters relating to his new religion and to God. His burning of his verse was more symbolic than an actual holocaust, for Hopkins was aware that several of his friends had kept copies of his poems, particularly his best friend at Oxford and future poet laureate of England, Robert Bridges.

Hopkins' ambivalence about writing verse is not difficult to understand. Thomas Merton felt that his own writing of poetry took time away from his real vocation: *contemplation.* Merton resolved his dilemma, however, writing that "contemplation has much to offer poetry. And poetry, in its turn, has something to offer contemplation....In understanding the relation of poetry to contemplation the first thing that needs to be stressed is the essential dignity of aesthetic experience."[1] Both Hopkins and Merton had fallen into the trap of dualistic thinking, failing to see that, although the creation of beauty is an aesthetic experience, it is not antithetical to the religious life because the source of all beauty, as St. Augustine reminds us, is God.

Hopkins' early poetry, it should be mentioned, was simple, lyrical, and in the Romantic tradition. "Heaven-Haven (A nun takes the veil)" is a good example of the kind of poetry he was composing in the 1860s:

I have desired to go
    Where springs not fail,
To fields where flies no sharp and sided hail
    And a few lilies blow.

And I have asked to be
    Where no storms come,
Where the green swell is in the havens dumb,
    And out of the swing of the sea.

This poetry is accessible as well as austerely beautiful; it indicates at an early time Hopkins' religious inclinations: he dreamt of a life of beauty where there is no "sharp and sided hail" and "no storms." His ideal land is not a geographical place, but a spiritual space where God abides, for only God is the spring that does "not fail." The poem also longs for withdrawal from the world; thus, it is prophetic, for Hopkins will indeed withdraw from the world to enter religious life, a life demanding that he sacrifice worldly pursuits and pleasures: as with Merton, his life would be dedicated to "God alone."

His sacrifice of composing poetry lasted until his time as a seminarian at St. Beuno College in Wales. On December 7, 1875, five Franciscan nuns died when the SS *Deutschland* was wrecked in a storm at the mouth of the Thames. Hopkins was emotionally moved. Soon after the wreck, St. Beuno's rector suggested to Hopkins that a poem should be written about the tragedy; his off-the-cuff comment was the spur Hopkins needed to resume writing poetry, which he had abandoned for seven years. Hopkins wrote his magnum opus, the ode *The Wreck of the Deutschland*, completing it by June of 1876. His poem was new, strange, and innovative: rich with startling images, strange and distorted syntax, and prolonged alliteration; fraught with ideas compressed and stretched to the breaking point—in short, he had introduced into the English language a new, modern idiom that had never before been read or *heard*, for Hopkins firmly believed that poetry should be read aloud, as all poetry should be, for it is not only a visual art form but also, primarily, an auditory one. (Although not a musician, Hopkins later in his life composed music. One of his finest poems is addressed to, and titled after, the composer Henry Purcell.)

Hopkins' poetry broke radically with old, traditional verse: his diction was seemingly fractured and strained, his grammar mirrored common speech, and his meter was the little-used "sprung rhythm," which had remained unnamed and undeveloped until Hopkins. All these things caught the eyes of early twentieth-century poets such as T. S. Eliot and W. H. Auden, and greatly influenced their efforts to escape pre—World War I formalism and to express the sensibilities of a weary generation sickened by the hypocrisy they saw all around them in politics, religion, and economics.

But Hopkins' poetry was too ahead of his time. His friends, particularly Robert Bridges, found *The Wreck* bizarre and incomprehensible. The Society of Jesus refused to publish it in its magazine *The Month*, which was a piercing and never-forgotten disappointment for Hopkins.

Robert Bridges maintained a lifetime correspondence with Hopkins. Sadly, Hopkins was never able to convince his friend to appreciate his poetry. Bridges must have seen genius in the work, however, for he kept copies of every poem his friend sent to him. Long after Hopkins' death of typhoid in Dublin in 1889, Bridges finally had his friend's poetry published in 1918.

The years after World War I were ripe for the publication of Hopkins' work. It was the beginning of the modern period of poetry, the romanticism of an earlier age defeated by the horror of World War I. Although he was a child of the Victorian age, many critics saw in Hopkins a modern poet who mirrored their concerns and enthusiasms, especially in regard to language. What have been labeled his "Terrible Sonnets," in particular, spoke to the postwar generation because the poems are filled with feelings of doubt, uncertainty, and despair, the very sentiments felt by so many young men who had survived the Great War yet were unable to discover any meaning in it.

By the 1930s, Gerard Manley Hopkins was considered a major English poet; his spiritually charged poetry spoke to the men and women who had endured the "war to end all wars" but were now caught in a worldwide economic depression. In short, his verse reflected their brief, periodic joys, as well as their increasing anguish in being alive in a century that to them seemed doomed (note T. S. Eliot's *The Waste Land*).

Which brings us to a question: Why is it that today so much attention is being lavished upon this priest-poet? There is a best-selling novel about him, Ron Hansen's *Exiles*, as well as a best-selling biography, *Gerard Manley Hopkins: A Life*, by Paul Mariani. Two symposiums devoted to his life and work are held annually in Ireland, and hundreds of dissertations are devoted to him each year.

Surely one of the reasons for the current interest is the so-called Terrible Sonnets. These heartrending sonnets are described as "terrible" because Hopkins was so grievously unhappy during his years at

University College in Dublin (1884—89). We must keep in mind that these are his last poems and in some ways are not characteristic of his opus; in fact, much of his poetry before Dublin are poems of joy in the beauty of God's world, although these too are tinged by melancholy. The Dublin sonnets, however, are fraught with angst, depression, despair, and suicidal thoughts. He bared his soul in these poems; one of them, he wrote to Bridges, was written as in blood. One of the most famous of these sonnets is "Carrion Comfort." Here are the first three lines:

Not, I'll not, carrion comfort, Despair, not feast on thee;
Not untwist—slack they may be—these last strands of man
In me ór, most weary, cry *I can no more.* I can.

These lines reveal a man struggling not to allow despair to achieve victory over him. The reader's heart goes out to him as he fights, even though he is most weary from combat not to give in, not to surrender to the "carrion comfort" of despair, a state of being that many critics have described as his "dark night of the soul" (not to be interpreted in the sense that St. John of the Cross meant).

Today people who suffer from depression see in Hopkins a mirror image of themselves. Yet, he offers them hope and consolation because he somehow survived his dark night of self-pity, self-loathing, and suicidal ideation. He overcame these suicidal thoughts and mustered the strength to "*not* choose not to be" (my emphasis).

There is also the personality of Gerard Manley Hopkins. He comes across to readers both in his poetry and in his journals and letters as a man of exquisite sensitivity, a person who found the beauty of God's world exhilarating. And he found beauty everywhere: in the variegated cracks of ice, the sheen and shape of a leaf, the colors of mist, the variety of sky blues, the convolutions of gliding clouds gilded by the sun, even the common wild parsley, its rue and cut.

He was also a charming man, his winning personality captured in his letters to his family and to friends like Robert Bridges and Canon Dixon, a former teacher at Highgate who was also a poet and who corresponded with Hopkins for most of his adult life. With Bridges, Hopkins revealed his toughness as well as his vulnerability; it hurt him that his friend could not appreciate his poetry. In a letter to Bridges, Hopkins reminded his friend that love should soften his criticism of his verse and his religion, a heartbreaking plea. Canon Dixon, on the other hand, openly discerned Hopkins' genius, even offering to have a few of Hopkins' poems included in an anthology, a generous gesture the poet refused.

Finally, Hopkins was a good man, with a shining holiness that sparkles in his sermons and his devotional writings. He dearly loved Jesus Christ, and he tried to the best of his ability to be Christlike. It is moving to read about the poet's ascetic practices, especially his practice of "custody of the eyes," when he would deny himself the sight of the beauty of the world, a sacrifice he gladly offered to God. For a poet, is there any greater sacrifice?

Hopkins' faith was centered on Christ. His intimacy with Christ is both touching and inspiring. In a sermon delivered in 1879, he wrote:

> Our Lord Jesus Christ, my brethren, is our hero, a hero all the world wants....He is a warrior and a conqueror of whom it is written he went forth conquering and to conquer. He is a king, Jesus of Nazareth king of the Jews....He is the true-love and the bridegroom of men's souls.[2]

It is poignant to read one of his sermons in which the poet gave a detailed description of Christ's appearance. It is not historical, but it reveals how real Christ was to Hopkins, and what he hoped Christ had looked like. Hopkins saw Jesus Christ not only in his imagination but everywhere he looked, as illustrated in his poem that begins "As kingfishers catch fire, dragonflies draw flame":

Í say móre: the just man justices;
    Kéeps gráce: thát keeps all his goings graces;
Acts in God's eye what in God's eye he is—
    Christ. For Christ plays in ten thousand places,
Lovely in limbs, and lovely in eyes not his
    To the Father through the features of men's faces.

Intellectually brilliant, charming, vulnerable, Hopkins was also a practical joker, once blowing pepper through a keyhole to cause his brothers on the other side of the door to sneeze. However, he remains in many ways an enigma. Although he diligently kept journals, they rarely address his inner life; his entries usually describe a beauty that captured him. In his letters he was guarded because he did not want his family or friends worrying about him. Bridges, for example, loathed the Jesuits and felt their way of life had grievously harmed his friend; thus, personal matters Hopkins might have shared, had Bridges been more tolerant, he chose not to share in order to discourage his friend's disparaging comments, not only about his poetry, but about the Jesuits and his Catholic faith. Thus, Hopkins was essentially a lonely man, keeping his true self sequestered in the dark.

We do have his poetry, however, and artists, even when they think they are in control of what they create, are influenced by another factor: the unconscious mind. Therefore, to those who have eyes to see and ears to hear, his poetry offers the fullest portrait of Gerard Manley Hopkins.

Walking with Gerard Manley Hopkins explores the life of Hopkins through all the genres he employed as a writer: poems, journals, letters, and devotional writings. It is our hope that the reader will win a deeper understanding of one of our greatest poets, a poet whose posthumous fame continues to grow and to attract new readers throughout the world, for he is indeed a poet for all people and for all seasons, definitely a poet for modern people, young and old. Christopher Ricks, one of our best contemporary critics, writes:

> If one wonders how the original readers of Hopkins—whether they were his friends, like Bridges, or whether they were his first readers in 1918, thirty years after his death—how they could have missed what Hopkins himself calls "the roll, the rise, the carol, the creation," one answer must surely be that the verse seemed to them to move so strangely. They perhaps could see that it bristled with life, but it seemed to bristle with difficulties, too.[3]

It is not always easy, we should warn readers, to understand Hopkins' verse; it takes effort, but we believe, along with T. S. Eliot, that poetry communicates even when we do not completely understand it. What we as readers need do is simply to be open to Hopkins' genius, and gradually, with reading and further reading, the beauty and meaning of his words will be revealed.

First Reading of
Gerard Manley Hopkins

Summer again! If we can call this rainy, cold season summer. It's time for me to write another "Walking with" book. I'm excited because Gerard Manley Hopkins (1844—89) is one of my favorite poets.

I first encountered Hopkins' poetry during my junior year of high school (the same year I first read Thomas Merton); several of his poems were included in our Catholic anthology, including "God's Grandeur," which begins, "The world is charged with the grandeur of God. / It will flame out, like shining from shook foil; / It gathers to a greatness, like the ooze of oil / Crushed."

What immediately struck me when I first read this poem was the poet's joy, if not ecstasy, in the beauty of God's creation. Furthermore, he was a priest, a Jesuit no less. I had been an altar boy for Jesuits in my parish ever since I was in the seventh grade and felt a bond with the poet because of it. I also loved poetry; even the difficult verse of T. S. Eliot couldn't diminish my enjoyment of verse. "God's Grandeur" was not as difficult as Eliot's "The Love Song of J. Alfred Prufrock," but its imagery was as startling and captivating. I was hooked even though I suspected that I had not caught all the nuances of Hopkins' poem. I certainly did not understand his concepts of *inscape* and *instress* (more about this later), which our teacher didn't explain, likely deciding to let us grasp the top-layered meaning of the poem now and tackle its deeper meaning in college.

Came across this commentary about "God's Grandeur" in a book left to me by a friend who recently died:

When Hopkins says that "the world is charged with the grandeur of God," his faith connects the "greatness" of nature with "the dearest freshness deep down things." And this freshness lives "because the Holy Ghost over the bent world broods with warm breast and with ah! bright wings." The holiness is not hidden to faith, but it takes faith to conclude that, behind or within, "this piece-bright paling shuts the spouse Christ home, Christ and his mother all his hallows" (the latter quotation from "The Starlight Night"). His world is not only ontologically deep and inhabited, it is theologically and biblically inhabited as well.[1]

The above analysis is one that high school students would likely not appreciate, and, if offered to them, it might indeed turn them off poetry!

More rain. Friends and relatives in Ireland and England rhapsodize in e-mails about their lyrical summer weather, its sunshine, warmth, and its unseasonable lack of rain, while we here in New England have rain every other day. It seems that we have swapped our lovely summer weather for Ireland and England's mist and rain. Is global warming the culprit?

Back to "God's Grandeur": I was instantly drawn to the word *God* in the poem's title. As a pious young man considering priesthood, I was excited by a world "charged" with God's grandeur, for it reinforced my sacramental perspective of creation, one nurtured in me by my Catholic education. For a Victorian poet like Hopkins, the electrical imagery was

14

an innovative if not a radical take on the world. The image of gold foil was also startlingly imaginative and eye-catching; I could delightfully conjure a sheet of shaken foil reflecting the sunlight and thus becoming a dazzling emblem of God, one proclaiming, "I am the Light of the world." The striking simile of oozing oil implied so many secular and sacred associations: olive oil, one of life's staples, especially in biblical times—also used for cleansing and healing wounds; also a sacred element in Catholic liturgies; also used to anoint priests, bishops, and kings, as well as the dying in the last rites of what was then called Extreme Unction. (The latter phrase dates me!)

A child of the Cold War, I was aware that humankind possessed the power to destroy itself and the world. I also understood Hopkins' anguish about our world being "bleared," "smeared," and wearing "man's smudge" and sharing "man's smell." As a teenager, I understood how much we had ravaged Mother Earth to a far greater degree than the Victorians had done; thus, Hopkins' anxiety about the earth moved me because he viewed it (as I do) as God's gift to us. Not only is nature God's gift to us; it is also a form of revelation: if we learn to "read" the world by paying close attention to it, we may catch divine glimpses; thus, to paraphrase Hopkins, we can confidently say that the "world is charged with the *meaning* of God." And part of the meaning of God's grandeur implies God's beauty and presence. Hopkins was surely aware of St. Augustine's teaching that God is the source of all beauty; thus, to see beauty appreciatively is a divine glimpse.

Before Hopkins became a Jesuit, he had already developed his concepts of *inscape* and *instress*. Following art critic John Ruskin's advice to observe nature closely, Hopkins indeed observed a thing's externality, but he also developed the notion that everything was unique by a quality it possessed within, what Aquinas described as the essence of a thing. But essence was seemingly an insufficient a term for Hopkins

15

(thus his later preference for Duns Scotus' theology); consequently, his concept of *inscape* encompasses both inward beauty and outward beauty; the latter, to Hopkins, was proof of an inward beauty. *Inscape* is unique unto itself, the *thisness* of a thing or its *isness*: Scotus' Latin term is *haecceitas*. Therefore, the kind of seeing that allows someone to discern a thing in all its distinctiveness is a sacred kind of seeing because the perceiver partakes of creation's holiness; for, as William Blake reminds us, "Every thing that lives is holy" (*Visions of the Daughters of Albion*).

On Hopkins and holiness, critic Ralph Harper says:

To Gerard Manley Hopkins holiness is only half hidden, and whatever is unconcealed is glorious. In poem after poem, he remarks on what he called the "instress" of nature, the inner energy, the anonymous presence of God. When we see beauty in nature or in persons, we glimpse the indwelling being of God, without which not only would there be no glory, there would be no individual reality, no "inscape" or individual form. The mind may be satisfied not to probe, to be content with seeing without supposing, acknowledging the beauty of form, effulgence of energy. But if not content, it can as Christian poets and theologians do—Hopkins the chief among them—penetrate the underlayment of material being to the energy of spirit, making it real, alive, or lovely.[2]

Like *inscape*, *instress* is another of Hopkins' self-coined words to express his concepts. *Instress* suggests the receptivity of the perceiver to receive the stress or the imprint of beauty experienced. It permits the perceiver to be "stressed"—that is, the observer is awed or astonished or surprised by the *instress* of a thing. In fact, the observer may possibly experience a wonder that blossoms into ecstasy. In such a state, there is a loss of the self (ego); thus, being lost in something other is similar to being lost in God, the fountain of beauty.

Hopkins found corroboration for his terms *inscape* and *instress* in a commentary by medieval Franciscan theologian Duns Scotus on the *Sentences of St. Peter Lombard.* Hopkins first came across Scotus in 1872 as a scholastic (student of philosophy) at the Jesuits' Stonyhurst library; he was delighted to discover that the late-thirteenth-century Franciscan's philosophy about form coincided with his own. Hopkins wrote:

> At this time I had first begun to get hold of the copy of Scotus on the Sentences in the Baddely library and was flushed with a new stroke of enthusiasm. It may come to nothing or it may be a mercy from God. But just then when I took in any inscape of the sky or sea I thought of Scotus.[3]

Scotus likely chose the Latin word *haecceitas* as a pun because it contains within it the medieval Latin word *ecceitas*, from *ecce*, meaning "Look!" or "Behold!" Looking at the world was for Hopkins more than a pastime but, rather, a major occupation: he soaked in the beauty of the world. Or, rather, he *beheld* the world, for "behold" suggests a deeper meaning than merely looking: it is the kind of seeing that becomes a part of one's being in an act of absolutely unmixed attention. It's the kind of seeing that William Blake wrote about in "Auguries of Innocence":

> To see a World in a grain of sand
> And a Heaven in a wild flower,
> Hold Infinity in the palm of your hand
> And Eternity in an hour.

I think of Christ's imperative, "Behold the lilies of the field"—his answer to the question of how to handle anxiety. Christ says that as God cares for the lilies, he will care for us. But there is for me a deeper significance: in beholding something "other," particularly something beautiful such as the lilies of the field, one enters a self-forgetting state of being, for when one truly beholds something, the observer and the observed become one. The "I" or the ego temporarily disappears and then returns only after the act of seeing; in that after-moment, we ponder what we have beheld. In such after-moments, art is often born, with poets quickly scribbling in their journals what they've just seen, their food for future writing; or painters quickly penciling drawings in sketch books, later to help in their painting.

Even now, many years after my first reading, I'm still moved by the relevance of "God's Grandeur." It has proved to be a prophetic poem, an early environmentalist poem, warning us that we have carelessly wreaked untold damage upon nature, but because our feet are "shod," we have lost *touch* with Mother Earth. Touch is a necessity in our lives; the poet Anne Sexton proclaims, "Touch is all" (from the poem "Rowing").

Just back from the garden where I cut full blooming peonies to place into a cut-glass vase. They are huge this year, likely because of all the rain. As to their beauty, well, I am certain that Hopkins could have captured their *inscape* in a poetic masterpiece. To behold with the eyes of a poet: oh, to be so gifted!

Sunday. The weatherman says we won't see the sun until Thursday! With school out, the kids won't be playing outside but inside, with their eyes glued to their computers. In the old days (I sound like an old fogey!), on such days I'd snuggle with a good book; today's young people don MP3 players or play computer games. The concept of play has dramatically changed: children used to play outside with their friends, but now they play indoors with machines. The streets of my neighborhood are eerily silent after school and on weekends. I remember a time when I'd hear the joyous raucousness of children playing, and mothers scolding their kids to come in because it was dinnertime.

On that note, a recent newspaper article told of a new position created by our school system: a professional is to be hired for the purpose of teaching children how to play! I wonder what the title is— Director of Play? What have we done to our children?

My high-school diary records that, along with "God's Grandeur," we read in class "Thou Art Indeed Just, Lord," in which the poet describes himself as a "eunuch," a word I had to look up. I was also puzzled by the poem's despair, in particular by its last line: "Oh thou lord of life, send my roots rain."

Later on, I wondered what had happened to the poet between writing the joyous paean to "God's Grandeur" and the despair-filled "Thou Art Indeed Just, Lord." I hadn't known during my first reading that the latter was considered one of the Terrible Sonnets. I surely understood that the poem revealed that Hopkins was an unhappy man. However, it didn't fit in with my image of a priest: I viewed priests as happy men who had willingly sacrificed their lives for God; I assumed that one of the spiritual gifts of their sacrifice was that God would compensate them with holiness and peace of mind.

Such naiveté!

And yet if one reads Hopkins' early poetry carefully, that written before his conversion, it suggests that he had his moments of depression. For instance, in the poem "Nondum," Hopkins writes:

My hand upon my lips I lay;
The breast's desponding sob I quell;
I move along life's tomb-decked way
And listen to the passing bell
Summoning men from speechless day
To death's more silent, darker spell.

The telling phrase is "desponding sob I quell." A sociable man and a notorious practical joker, Hopkins could be overcome by depression when his natural creative bent was frustrated or not recognized. When he arrived in Dublin, Ireland, where he found himself among total strangers and where his teaching workload overwhelmed him, depression finally got the upper hand and nearly destroyed him.

I can't believe it: Hail and a rainstorm predicted for tomorrow.

When I first taught "God's Grandeur" to my high school juniors, one of my brightest students questioned me about why a religious poem was included in a public school curriculum. I was surprised by his query, and for a moment I wondered if I had stepped over the division between church and state, but I remembered that we were using an anthology approved by the city's school committee.

I had to think quickly, and although I don't remember my exact words, I said something like this: "If we can read the poetry concerning Matthew Arnold's agnosticism ('Dover Beach'), of Alfred Lord Tennyson's beleaguered faith ('In Memoriam'), and of Thomas Hardy's pessimism ('The Darkling Thrush'), why can we not read the poetry of a man of faith?"

I don't remember my student's response but retain a vague impression that my answer proved satisfactory, for there ensued no debate.

I didn't fully explore Hopkins' poetic opus until I was in college. My delayed exploration was likely the result of my fascination with the life and work of Thomas Merton, whom I had adopted as my spiritual mentor. During my junior and senior years in high school, I devoured Merton's books. When I noticed that Merton had hoped to write his dissertation at Columbia on Hopkins, a poet he greatly admired, I decided that Hopkins definitely deserved a revisit. The fact that both men had converted to Catholicism was an added attraction: I was always fascinated by Catholic converts, such as Graham Greene, Edith Sitwell, Siegfried Sassoon, and Evelyn Waugh. Also, I had been warned by my teachers to read books that would bolster, not harm, my Catholic faith, and to my then conservative Catholic mind, Merton and Hopkins were safe to read and thus no threat to my faith. To be candid, however, as a cradle Catholic I believed I understood Catholicism better than these two converts, whose first fervor, although charming to note in their work, was easily spotted. But in time, I began to respect their sincere embracing of the Catholic faith: these men truly believed in Catholicism: it had become their whole life.

The concept of escaping from life is quite noticeable in Hopkins' pre-conversion poetry. A good example of this is found in his poem "The Habit of Perfection":

Elected Silence, sing to me
And beat upon my whorlèd ear,
Pipe me to pastures still and be
The music that I care to hear.

What Hopkins and Merton shared, although they loved the beauty of the world, was *contemptus mundi* (a contempt of the world). Merton admits to this contempt in his journals, viewing the world as evil. Hopkins is more oblique, as he is in "The Habit of Perfection." Both men believed that as human beings they could be perfected if they joined the one, true Church. Both men discovered, however, that on joining the Church, they were still themselves. This came as a surprise, for I feel they believed that they would be totally transformed into a more perfect person. But that's not how it works in life. The great lesson that so many must learn is that peace of mind comes not so much from perfection (an impossible ideal) but from self-acceptance. Merton learned this truth early enough in his short life to experience some years of spiritual and psychological peace. Hopkins never stopped believing in perfection, and this, I believe, was one of the causes of his episodes of depression. As his journals clearly show, it surely must have been frustrating for him to have to return again and again to his spiritual counselor to confess the same sins; the very sins that haunted him as a youth were the same ones that plagued him in his forties.

Interesting coincidence: Evelyn Waugh edited Merton's autobiography for its British publication, and he rejected Merton's title, *The Seven Storey Mountain*, and chose, instead, Hopkins' phrase "Elected Silence."

Reading through Hopkins' poetry, I had to struggle with his difficult diction, his strange syntax, and his unusual rhythm. It took a while to understand his sprung rhythm, a metrical system resembling natural speech, consisting in scanning by accents alone or stresses alone so that in a foot there may be one strong syllable or it may be many light and one strong. Regardless of the difficulties, however, Hopkins did communicate with me. T. S. Eliot once observed that even if we don't completely understand a poem, it can still communicate with us. So the lines of communication were surely open, but when I arrived at Hopkins' last poems, those that have commonly become known as the Terrible Sonnets, I was, to be candid, astonished by their apparent despair. When I had read them all together as a unit (six of them), I was puzzled and disturbed that Hopkins, usually a poet of praise and joy, now appeared to be a poet filled with self-pity, self-loathing, a man who had perhaps even entertained the idea of suicide—perhaps cursorily, but the idea had been a consideration.

What happened to Hopkins when he left England for Dublin to teach at University College, where he composed his Terrible Sonnets?

His Terrible Sonnets reveal a man naked in his pain, a man lonely, lamenting his life. Why such despair? Why depressed? Why suicidal? Hopkins was a priest, a man of faith who had dedicated his life to God. Surely such a man finds consolation and peace of mind in Christ, in God.

The Terrible Sonnet I struggled most with as a young man was "Carrion Comfort." Here was a Hopkins who puzzled me. He was battling despair, yet he offered no specific reason for the cause of his despair. He was weary, but he prodded himself to "untwist" the "last strands" of manhood in him to fight back despair, to hope for day to come and to choose to be and *not* choose not to be, an echo of Hamlet's famous soliloquy "To be or not to be," which is a meditation on whether or not to live or to take one's life.

The fact that Hopkins could muster the will and energy to write about his spiritual and psychological condition I found encouraging. Writing had always been an outlet for Hopkins (journals, verse, letters, sermons, devotional notebooks), and although there was a period of his life, roughly seven years, in which he didn't write much verse, he always kept a journal. (Why he stopped maintaining his personal journal remains a mystery, for like Merton he was an inveterate diarist.) His journal entries are not deep accounts of his inner life—that was put into his verse—but they allowed him to focus on something other than himself; thus, for the most part his journals are filled with descriptions of nature. Nevertheless, the journals had been an important outlet for the poet, providing him a haven ("Heaven-Haven") of escape from the I, the ego.

Hopkins did, however, reveal more of his inner life in his letters to friends. For example, after a year in Ireland he disclosed to his lifelong friend A.W. M. Baillie that the melancholy to which he had always been prone had lately become "rather more distributed, constant, and crippling." Among its manifestations was "daily anxiety about work to be done." In his worst moments, he compared his state to madness. He even admitted, "I see no ground for thinking I shall ever get over it or ever succeed in doing anything that is not forced on me to do of any consequence."[4]

This admission is quite revelatory. When Hopkins employs the word *melancholy*, he is referring to what we of the twenty-first century mean by depression. One of the best accounts of depression in our time is *Darkness Visible*, written by William Styron. Styron did not particularly like the modern term *depression*, preferring instead the word *melancholy* to describe his crippling depression, which nearly caused him to take his life. He wrote:

Depression, most people know, used to be termed "melancholia," a word which appears in English as early as the year 1303 and crops up more than once in Chaucer, who in his usage seemed to be aware of its pathological nuances. "Melancholia" would still appear to be a far more apt and evocative word for the blacker forms of the disorder, but it was usurped by a noun with a bland tonality and lacking any magisterial presence, used indifferently to describe an economic decline or a rut in the ground, a true wimp of a word for such a major illness.[5]

Hopkins admits to being a victim of melancholia, and with his exquisite sensitivity to words, he surely meant what he said. And it was not a minor illness; it is, as Styron states, a "major illness." Despite his bouts of depression, Hopkins seemingly never allowed even his "blacker forms" to triumph over him. As to suicide, he rejected it. As to his reasons for not taking his life, they may well have been similar to Hamlet's reasons for not taking his life: the alternative was far worse than present reality, for suicides were damned to hell for eternity, and Hopkins believed in a literal hell; it was as real as the world he lived in.

Some critics and biographers claim that the Terrible Sonnets reflect Hopkins' "dark night of the soul," part of a five-stage mystical journey: awakening, purgation, illumination, dark night of the soul, and union. During the dark night, a mystic must endure God's absence. Evelyn Underhill wrote:

This is the period of spiritual confusion and impotence, the last drastic purification of the whole character, the re-making of personality in accordance with the demands of the transcendent sphere, which is called by some mystics the Dark Night of the Soul, by others the "spiritual death," or "purgation of the will." Whatever the psychological causes which produce it, all mystics agree that this state constitutes a supreme moral crisis, in which the soul is finally cleansed of all attachments to self-hood, and utterly surrendered to the purposes of the Divine life. Spiritual man is driven from his old paradise, enters on a new period of struggle, must evolve "another story to his soul."[6]

In his Terrible Sonnets, Hopkins rails at God, complains to God, even whines to God, but God is as real and present to him as are his Dublin students and colleagues; thus, I don't believe his poems are illustrative of a mystical "dark night" that entails a sense of the *absence* of God. The term "dark night of the soul" is St. John of the Cross's expression for a portion of the mystic's journey to God, but I don't believe that Hopkins was a mystic; therefore, to apply the term "dark night of the soul" to him, as some critics do, is misleading. God is still with him (although, he admits, "distant"). At the end of "Carrion Comfort," Hopkins realizes that during his period of darkness, he's indeed "wrestling with (my God!) my God." Earlier in the poem, he anthropomorphizes Despair and asks it, "Why wouldst thou rude on me / Thy wring-world right foot rock?"

What had brought Hopkins to this state? The only way to answer my question meant a close reading not only of his verse but also of his journals, letters, and devotional writings, which I've done for many years. I also read five scholarly biographies and various commentaries. I finally developed my own theory about what had led him to the brink of the abyss.

This summer I will reappraise my theory about what triggered Hopkins' bouts of depression, for I believe it's more complicated than his simply being a melancholic. I also need to explore areas of his life into which I only cursorily looked. My summer "walking with Hopkins" will, I believe, win for me a deeper understanding of this remarkable man, who happens to be a famous and admired poet as well as a Catholic priest.

One thing I have no doubt about: Hopkins changed the way I look at the world, and anyone who can produce such a miracle deserves gratitude—thus, this journal will also serve as my thank-you to him. It was Hopkins who taught me to be attentive to the world, to see it as a reflection of God's beauty. Some critics may say he simply saw the world as it is, but I believe he saw more than the thing itself: he discerned divine glimpses everywhere, and in my opinion they enliven his verse. For a reader like me, they confirm my faith and hope in Christ.

Another reason for revisiting Hopkins' life and work is that I want to conduct Hopkins retreats. Having directed Merton and Nouwen retreats for several years, I'm now ready for something new and challenging. How can Hopkins help us in our spiritual lives? How can he help us become more intimate with God? In short, how can he help us become better Christians?

Like Simone Weil, the French mystic-philosopher-writer, I have always felt that the beauty of poetry can lure (she employs the word *snare*) people to God, for God is the source of beauty. Hopkins' poetry is certainly beautiful, but it is also overtly Christian; therefore, it appeals to many people of faith, both Catholic and non-Catholic, and I would feel honored to introduce Hopkins to people who have never read him.

I am amazed by the number of Catholics who do not realize that one of the greatest of our modern poets is a Catholic. And Hopkins is, I feel, a modern poet, more of the twentieth century than the nineteenth; his poetic style is certainly not Victorian, and his Terrible Sonnets are more in line with modern existentialism than with Victorian Darwinism. Too many critics have stated that no spiritual poetry has been written since the nineteenth century. Such a remark is absurd. I can think of several "spiritual" poets off the top of my head: T. S. Eliot, W. H. Auden, Edith Sitwell, R. S. Thomas, Thomas Merton, Richard Wilbur, Franz Wright, Kathleen Norris, Mary Oliver, Marie Ponsot, and many others.

I've just read Hopkins' first surviving poem, "The Escorial," a fine poem for a fifteen-year-old boy:

There is a massy pile above the waste
Amongst Castilian barrens mountain-bound;
A sombre length of grey; four towers placed
At corners flank the stretching compass round;
A pious work with threefold purpose crown'd—
A cloister'd convent first, the proudest home
Of those who strove God's gospel to confound
With barren rigour and a frigid gloom—
Hard by a royal palace and a royal tomb.

The poem reveals that he learned much from Tennyson and that he was already a master of rhyme. With it, he won his school's poetry prize. It's remarkable that the boy Hopkins was already devotedly composing poetry, which makes it even more amazing that he later renounced writing verse: during his first seven years as a Jesuit he wrote only two poems in honor of the Blessed Mother. We are ever indebted to Robert Bridges, who saved all of the verse Hopkins had sent to him for comment. The Jesuits burned many of the poet's papers at Hopkins' death. One wonders if there were treasures lost in the holocaust, not only poetry but also diaries and other writings. This possibility has haunted me, and it's the basis of my novella *The Secret Dublin Diary of Gerard Manley Hopkins.*

I've always been fascinated with diaries. My first work of fiction, *The Lost Diary of Francis Thompson*, was based on the theory that Francis Thompson, who composed "The Hound of Heaven," had kept a diary that somehow was lost (he actually *had* kept a diary, but it was never found). The diary is the genre I feel most comfortable with. Usually writers of diaries are maskless; thus, we have the opportunity to meet and know the real person. Some diarists, however, are too self-conscious about their diaries being published in the future; thus, they carefully craft them, consequently losing spontaneity and authenticity. This is true of Thomas Merton's first published diaries (the later unexpurgated diaries are much more "real" and revelatory). It's also true of André Gide and May Sarton: they wrote for an audience. The exception to the rule is Henri Nouwen: I believe he was one of the most transparent diarists I've ever read. Because he was so vulnerably himself, I immensely enjoy reading his diaries, for I feel I am meeting the man as he truly was, a person without masks. His diaries seem to say, "Here I am, and do what you will—take me or leave me."

The Genesee Diary is the first Nouwen diary I read, an account of his time spent at Genesee Abbey in upstate New York. He felt that his life had become too frenetic with teaching, lecturing, and writing books at the expense of his prayer life. He understood that he needed more silence and solitude in his life, and he also entertained the idea of becoming a Trappist, as had Merton, whom Nouwen considered his spiritual mentor. At Genesee, being an inveterate writer, Nouwen began to keep a daily journal. At the urging of friends, he later published it. It was an enormous success, catapulting Nouwen from the second tier of writers on modern spirituality into the first. And his life was never again the same, for he achieved more fame than ever before.

As to his becoming a Trappist, Abbot John Eudes Bamberger advised Nouwen that he was not suited for monastic life. His ministry, Bamberger counseled, was one of reaching out to people with the message of the Gospel through his teaching, preaching, and spiritual direction. Nouwen agreed, but he did again stay at Genesee once more for nearly seven months. At Genesee, Nouwen was able to quiet down, and in the silence and solitude of the abbey, he was recharged to face the demands of his rather busy life as a teacher and author.

Like Hopkins, Merton considered poetry frivolous when juxtaposed to his religious life. As with Hopkins, it was Merton's superior who "saved" his writing career by ordering him to write his autobiography; for Hopkins, it was his rector who suggested, not ordered, that he write a poem about the wreck of the SS *Deutschland*.

What's puzzling is that, for such brilliant men, neither of them seemingly realized that his talent to write was a God-given gift; not to nurture it was against the biblical injunction not to hide one's light under a bushel. For the Jesuit Hopkins, the dilemma was particularly ironic: a pivotal line from St. Ignatius's *Spiritual Exercises* is *Homo creatus est laudare*: "[Humanity] is created to praise." Is there a better way to praise God than through poetry? And if either man needed a model to emulate, he need only open his Bible and read the psalms, a collection of some of the world's greatest poetry—fully directed at God.

Still thinking about Hopkins and Merton.

They both believed that the quickest way to God was by the route of penance: the harder one was on oneself—by fasting, by custody of the eyes, even by flagellating the flesh—the holier the sacrifice. (It is likely that both men practiced self-flagellation at some point in their religious lives, since it was common to the Jesuit and Trappist orders. This ascetic practice has not completely disappeared from our modern world; it has recently been revealed that Pope John Paul II flagellated himself as a penance.)

The concept of *agape*, God's unconditional love for each of us, was not widely propagated in Hopkins' time, and even today many Christians consider it almost too good to be true. There still exists in many Christian minds the Calvinistic idea that God is out to zap us, to punish us for our sins. But agape is true! And if Hopkins had truly believed in it, the Terrible Sonnets may never have been written, but he was imbued with the idea of Christ as both Judge and Savior, with an emphasis on the former rather than the latter.

Religion is not static; it fortunately evolves. But even today in certain circles of Christianity, it is daring to speak of agape. So many Christians still believe that they have to *earn* salvation by subjecting themselves to deprivations as if they had to convince God that they are worthy. They should read Lady Julian of Norwich, who reminds us that with God there is no blame, only love, and that "all shall be well." For me the "word icon" that most eloquently speaks this truth is George Herbert's poem "Love (iii)":

Love bade me welcome, yet my soul drew back,
    Guilty of dust and sin
But quick-eyed Love, observing me grow slack
    From my first entrance in,
Drew nearer to me, sweetly questioning
    If I lack'd any thing.

"A guest," I answer'd, "worthy to be here";
    Love said, "You shall be he."
"I, the unkind, ungrateful? Ah, my dear,
    I cannot look on thee."
Love took my hand, and smiling did reply,
    "Who made the eyes but I?"

31

"Truth, Lord, but I have marr'd them: let my shame
      Go where it doth deserve."
"And know you not," says Love, "who bore the blame?"
      "My dear, then I will serve."
"You must sit down," says Love, "and taste my meat."
      So I did sit and eat.

Hopkins had two fathers: his birth father, Manley Hopkins, owner of a marine insurance company, and John Henry Newman, his spiritual father, one of the greatest intellectuals of the nineteenth century, as well as a convert to the Catholic faith, later to be named a cardinal. When Hopkins converted to Catholicism, he "lost" his birth father. To be sure, his father never forbade his son entry into his home, even though the rift was never completely healed, although Hopkins rarely returned home once he became a Jesuit. His mother and his six siblings were also aghast by his conversion; therefore, his relationship to his whole family was forever changed by his departure from the Church of England to embrace Catholicism.

Although Newman, who had received Hopkins into the Church, was aware that the young convert was planning to enter a religious order, he never pressured Hopkins to become an Oratorian like himself. It would likely not have done any good to do so because Hopkins was his own man: his looks—he was small, with a sensitive, reflective face, fragility seemingly stamped upon it—belied his strength of character. And he was actually more attracted to the Jesuit order.

Founded in the sixteenth century by St. Ignatius of Loyola, the Jesuits were well known for the rigor of their Rule. But Hopkins was always drawn to the difficult. Perhaps his final decision to join the Jesuits was compensatory: he understood his fragility, thus he likely, unconsciously, rendered himself "manly" by choosing "the road not taken." Some critics have even theorized that he was occasionally subject to masochistic tendencies, which is something I must explore, for if I'm to understand the whole man, I must not be afraid to meet his "shadow," to use Jung's term: the shadow aspects of Hopkins' personality.

I've often wondered why Hopkins didn't become a Trappist; at the time they were the toughest of the tough when it came to religious orders. But perhaps it was because the Jesuits had won a reputation for intellectual rigor, since most of them advanced toward graduate studies. It was likely this aspect of the order that attracted the brilliant Hopkins (who won a first in the classics and philosophy at Balliol, Oxford). And yet one wonders whether the Jesuits were indeed the right order for a man with his kind of temperament. I believe that he might have been happier as a Franciscan, or perhaps a Benedictine; I'm speculating about this, of course, but others have thought the same. But the idea is moot: the fact is that he became a Jesuit.

The Jesuits have belatedly become quite proud of Hopkins, but when he was alive, they considered him an eccentric failure, and they didn't quite know how to dispatch him in their order. He should have become an academic in one of their colleges, but he ended up being sent to poor urban parishes in the midlands of England, because in his theological exams he favored Duns Scotus over Thomas Aquinas. Favoring Duns Scotus was a daring move on Hopkins' part, but one that marked him as unorthodox and thus conferred the kiss of death for advancement in the Society of Jesus. And he paid a high price for his "blunder" with a failing mark in theology: thus, he never became a professed Jesuit father, only attaining the lower status of "spiritual coadjutor," and would never move up the ladder of his order because of it. A "high price" seems perhaps to be an understatement. How his superiors and the Order itself failed to see the genius of Gerard

Manley Hopkins is a mystery to me. But again, it's a moot point, because today his genius and poetry are internationally known and loved. Even the man himself is loved and revered.

Hopkins spent years as a priest in poverty-stricken parishes; indeed, between 1877 and 1884, he was assigned to eleven different places. He was horrified by the squalor he witnessed. It seems to me that anyone who truly knew him and was aware of his intellectual brilliance (Benjamin Jowett, the eminent classics scholar and one of his tutors at Oxford, called him the "star of Balliol") would have realized that Hopkins, who had a loathing of the "sordidness" of things, could never have thrived in a poor urban parish. His biographer Paul Mariani suggests that Hopkins would have been appalled to hear the confessions of the poor and discover the vice to which poverty had reduced them. For a man prone to depression, such confessions could only have an insalubrious effect on him.

But Hopkins was obedient to his order, and, indeed, obedience is one of a Jesuit's vows. Frequent reassignments, often at very short notice, were common. A priest (or brother) might be sent anywhere that Jesuits were present. For Hopkins, it could have been the British Commonwealth or it could have been to the missions in another country. (My own childhood parish, for example, was a church established for immigrant German Catholics and staffed by Jesuits from Germany.)

Hopkins' position is reminiscent of Thomas Merton's. Because of his vow of obedience, Merton too had no autonomy, and because he chose to be ruled by an abbot, he obeyed him by remaining a monk at Gethsemani when he actually wanted to leave. In fact, many religious orders recruited Merton; it would have been a coup to have Merton live among them, but his abbot repeatedly counseled him that God wanted him at Gethsemani Abbey in Kentucky.

A contemporary of Hopkins commented as follows on the obedience to which Jesuits are vowed:

> The novice is taught to obey his superior without ever questioning the wisdom of the order given; the perfection of Jesuit obedience includes not only the obedience of the will, so that he does what is commanded promptly, bravely, and thoroughly, but also an obedience of the judgment, so that he regards what is commanded as the best thing possible for him....It is the habit, the difficult habit of abstaining from any mental criticism of the Society of Jesus.[7]

Why would such independent, strong-willed men like Hopkins and Merton choose to join such strict religious orders that demand absolute obedience from its members? Perhaps both men may have understood something about themselves that required obedience to an ideal, fearing in themselves a propensity toward self-harm if they were allowed complete freedom in their lives. This is only a speculation, but from what I've learned about the lives of both men, I believe this to be a distinct possibility.

Just recently at a retreat I directed, a retreatant asked me what would have happened to Thomas Merton had he not become a monk. I had to answer honestly so I said I believed that he may have remained in New York City to try to establish himself as a writer. Had he failed as a writer, he may have turned to drink. Merton liked to drink, and if he had considered himself a failure as a writer, he may have turned to alcohol as an escape. Some of Merton's biographers

35

have speculated that he was already on his way to developing an alcohol problem, but then his conversion occurred, followed by his admission into the Abbey of Gethsemani, both of which saved him in more ways than one.

One of my favorite Catholic poets, Marie Ponsot, had something illuminating to say about the Terrible Sonnets (I accidentally found this on the Internet) when she was asked about her relationship with Hopkins:

> Well, it changes over the years. There's a poem in the book [*Easy*, Ponsot's newest volume of verse] called "Thank Gerard." I have an intense, intense love of what they call the "Terrible Sonnets," the sonnets in which he keeps going in spite of being in...despair, really, or very close to the bottom of the pit of despair. He couldn't be as prayerful as he wanted to be, he couldn't experience prayer as anything but a deadly, isolating event, and he didn't quit. Ever. He complained, but he didn't say, "Well, this is not for me; this is no good." He had made a vow, in fact, that he would not quit, so he didn't. That act of being faithful to one's original intention is something that the twentieth century gradually gave up on. First we lost our contact with the reality of reality....That idea that "I have said I will, and so I do." And it's odd because, even though men have, and women have, varying degrees of success (not a lot of success) in keeping their word, they have made vows as far back as recorded history takes us, and they have felt themselves bound by those vows, even in betraying them.
>
> So it's something that the twentieth century threw out without even noticing.[8]

I also watched Marie Ponsot talk about Hopkins on *YouTube*. She read two new poems about him as well. They are wonderful poems. Today I went to the bookstore to purchase her new book. I want to have all of her books, for she is an important Catholic voice, often published in *Commonweal*. The poem I liked best is "Why Vow," which is about Hopkins.

With Ponsot's estimation of Hopkins I have no argument. Yes, he kept his vows, but let us not forget for a minute that it was difficult for him to do so. It likely demanded every ounce of his will not to break them. But as Ponsot says in her poem, "He did as he said." It's similar to saying a person is one of his word. What greater compliment can a person receive?

Conversion

First fervor is a well-known characteristic of converts, and Hopkins was no exception. He was likely more Roman than any other Catholic he had known. On entering the Jesuits, he burned his poetry because he thought it would interfere with his spiritual state and with his vocation. While this was drastic to say the least (he also destroyed one of his journals in June 1866), the import of his "slaughter" is diminished because he knew that several of his friends had kept copies of his poems. His act is surely an aspect of the first fervor of a convert, but there may also be something masochistic about it: it was a holocaust not only of his poems but also of a part of his inner self, of his personhood. Why such violence toward himself? And if he thought it would be pleasing to God to sacrifice what was dearest to him, a talent with which he was born, what was his concept of God?

Perhaps I shouldn't be perplexed by Hopkins' burning of his poems. Raised a Catholic before the Second Vatican Council, I could have easily sat down to dinner with Hopkins, and we would have shared the same beliefs and practices. Before he became a Catholic, he had already begun to follow what were then common Catholic asceticisms: fasting, inflicting punishment on himself, kissing the floor in front of an image of the Virgin Mary, daily noting his sins in a notebook, and going to confession often. Such acts I myself performed in preparation for my entry into the seminary (in the end I chose not to become a priest).

I too had frequently fasted and sacrificed small pleasures, like eating sweets, during Lent in order to please God (or was it to placate

God for my "many" sins when I was just a boy?). I too believed that the more difficult my spiritual asceticism, the more likely it would lead me to holiness; it's what my teachers (Franciscan nuns and Jesuit priests) had taught me. And like Hopkins, I too suffered from severe scrupulosity, examining each of my actions and thoughts to discover if I had indeed sinned, ever aware of God's omniscience, of God being aware of my every thought and act, and ever fearful that I could in an instant fall from a state of grace into sin, thereby endangering my immortal soul to the eternal flames of hell. I believed I could lose God and heaven by entertaining an impure thought for just a second or two, and how could one ever be *certain* that one's will had not consented to such temptations?

To live under such a threat of damnation was a fearful way to live—with anxiety, if not terror, a constant companion. I wasn't alone in my fear, for many of my friends, all of us products, as they say, of Catholic schools, from kindergarten to high school and sometimes college, felt the same way. Because of the emphasis on sin and its consequent sense of guilt, many of them fell away from the Church, never to return. As one friend said to me, "I never again want to hear a sermon about venial and mortal sins."

I had read James Joyce's *Portrait of an Artist as a Young Man*, a novel I highly identified with. The famous sermon on hell and damnation is one I recognized. Had I not as a young person heard similar sermons delivered by the Jesuits of my parish? (Interesting coincidence: James Joyce attended University College—where Hopkins spent his last years as a professor of classics—and lived in Newman House, the same house Hopkins lived in). Educated his whole life by Jesuits, Joyce seriously considered the idea of becoming one. Here is a portion of his famous hell-and-damnation sermon from his autobiographical *The Portrait of an Artist as a Young Man*:

Our earthly fire again, no matter how fierce or widespread it may be, is always of a limited extent: but the lake of fire in hell is boundless, shoreless and bottomless. It is on record that the devil himself, when asked the question by a certain soldier, was obliged to confess that if a whole mountain were thrown into the burning ocean of hell it would be burned up in an instant like a piece of wax. And this terrible fire will not afflict the bodies of the damned only from without but each lost soul will be a hell unto itself, the boundless fire raging in its very vitals. O, how terrible is the lot of those wretched beings! The blood seethes and boils in the veins, the brains are boiling in the skull, the heart in breast glowing and bursting, the bowels a redhot mass of burning pulp, the tender eyes flaming like molten balls.[1]

When I first taught this novel to public school students in the late 1970s, they were appalled by the sermon. Many of these students were Catholic, and I remember thinking that things had changed for the good after Vatican II. To bring young people to God, you don't have to scare the hell out of them literally; better to bring them to God by speaking of God's unconditional love for each of us.

In my own experience of twelve years of Catholic education, I never once heard of the concept of God's unconditional love. But I and many other Catholics heard plenty about sin and damnation in our youth. We cannot revise the past but we should not deny it. Religion was negatively presented in similar fashion to Protestants. And it is likely still being done today in various parts of the world.

What about Hopkins and hell? In his review of Paul Mariani's new biography on Hopkins, Adam Kirsch writes:

Hopkins, of course, believed quite literally in Hell. Mariani quotes the sermon on this subject which he delivered in 1882, and is as cruel and brutal as the famous hellfire sermon in "Portrait of the Artist as a Young Man." After reminding his parishioners that "there are dangers by land and sea, wrecks, railway accidents, lightnings, mischances with machinery, fires, falls...[and] murders," Hopkins goes on to evoke Hell as "the brimstone, the dregs and bilge-water of that pit," where the sinner's lusts become "like vomit and like dung." The odd echo of his own style in "mischances with machinery, fires, falls" only drives home the disparity between what Hopkins felt about the world and what he believed about it.[2]

The happiest period of Hopkins' life occurred during his time at Oxford. (Although he was happy at St. Beuno's College in Wales, he was plagued by poor health and depression; yet he transcended both by writing some of his most sublime poems while there.) Hopkins devotes two poems to Oxford: "To Oxford" and "Duns Scotus's Oxford." In the first he writes:

New-dated from the terms that reappear,
More sweet-familiar grows my love to thee,
And still thou bind'st me to fresh fealty
With long-superfluous ties, for nothing here
Nor elsewhere can thy sweetness unendear.

For the rest of his life, Hopkins would lovingly remember his days at Oxford. During his second year there, he had better quarters, with a bedroom, sitting room, and scout's hole, along with a new carpet and new wallpaper. On his walls hung portraits of Raphael, Shelley,

Keats, and Tennyson. He had scores of friends and enjoyed entertaining them, with breakfasts similar to today's wine-and-cheese parties. With them he went on walking tours, trips to Europe, and art exhibitions, and participated in stimulating conversations about God and theology; there was also much swimming, his favorite sport.

His Oxford tutor was Walter Pater, the high priest of "art for art's sake." Hopkins toyed with the idea of becoming a painter. In addition to his poetic gifts, he also possessed remarkable ability at drawing, as illustrated by the meticulous drawings found in his journals. Like two of his brothers, he might have been able to establish a career as an artist or illustrator.

Hopkins avidly read the work of art critic and theorist John Ruskin, whose *Modern Painters* was a widely influential work. Hopkins' journals are filled with drawings of architectural structures like Gothic windows, as well as of trees, plants, and sky. Ruskin influenced Hopkins' way of looking at the world, for Ruskin advocated an exquisitely close attention to the beauty of the English countryside; only by attention, he believed, would the English realize how much of their country's beautiful landscape had been destroyed by the Industrial Revolution.

Writing to his friend Alexander Baillie, Hopkins described his sketches as possessing "a Ruskinese point of view." He would experience "particular periods of admiration for particular things in Nature," such as being "astonished at the beauty of a tree," and when this feeling had worn off, it was "consigned to my treasury of explored beauty."[3]

When Hopkins was a student at Oxford, the Oxford Movement still lingered in the air, as did the presence of the charismatic John

Henry Newman. In fact, by the time Hopkins arrived at Oxford, Newman had become a legend. Matthew Arnold's famous description of Newman arriving at St. Mary's Church in Oxford to preach is worth recording here:

> Who could resist the charm of that spiritual apparition, gliding in the dim afternoon light through the aisles of St. Mary's, rising into the pulpit, and then, in the most entrancing of voices, breaking the silence with words and thoughts which were a religious music—subtle, sweet and mournful? Happy the man who in susceptible season of youth hears such voices! They are a possession to him forever.[4]

Hopkins was faithful about attending church on Sunday and receiving the Eucharist. He preferred High Church Anglicanism because it had adopted many of the Catholic rituals that had been discarded during the Dissolution begun by Henry VIII. Its religious services incorporated many of these customs: traditional eucharistic vestments, incense, unleavened bread for communion, six candles on the high altar, the celebration of the Eucharist facing eastward, the sign of the cross, and the mixing of sacramental wine with water. In addition, High Church Anglicans rang bells at the elevation of the host; used the word *Mass* to refer to the eucharistic liturgy; decorated their churches with statues of saints, pictures of religious scenes, and icons; and preserved other Catholic rituals such as liturgical processions, veneration of the Virgin Mary, the invocation of the saints, and Benediction of the Blessed Sacrament.

Hopkins also fervently believed in the Catholic dogma of the Real Presence, which he regarded as a "great aid to belief and object of belief." Without this, he declared, religion is "somber, dangerous, illogical"; with it, he said, it is "loveable. Hold that and you will gain all Catholic truth."[5]

Two of the most important events of Hopkins' life occurred at Oxford: converting to Catholicism and meeting Robert Bridges' cousin Digby Augustus Stewart Mackworth Dolben.

Dolben—like Hopkins, a young poet—entered Eton in January 1862. From 1863 onward, he seriously considered conversion to Roman Catholicism. In a spurt of enthusiasm for his new interest in Catholicism, Dolben—as Hopkins would do years later, and as poets have done with great drama reputedly as far back as Ovid and Plato—burned all his poems. This was during Lent 1864. Fortunately, a friend of Dolben's kept copies of this early verse—as Hopkins' friends would keep his—and thus they survived.

Dolben clandestinely met with several Catholic religious orders and in April 1864 joined the English Order of St. Benedict, founded by the Rev. Joseph Leycester Lynne. At this time, he began to emulate a medieval monk, wearing a habit and going barefoot whenever he could.

Dolben tried unsuccessfully to meet with John Henry Newman; however, Newman later corresponded with him about his wish to convert. As with Hopkins, Newman advised the young man to wait and not to act hastily. Newman understood full well that, although conversion can transfigure the life of the convert, it can shatter an English family—such high contempt had the English for the Catholic faith; a rather ironic fact when one considers that England had once been a Catholic country and Henry VIII had been dubbed the "Defender of the Faith."

It's interesting to note that John Henry Newman had taken the time to answer the letters of a nineteen-year-old. It shows that he was a caring, sensitive man who seriously considered young people's religious crises. Of course, the fact that Dolben was a member of one of the most distinguished families in England surely helped to prompt Newman's reply. Despite that, to his credit he must have handled the young man with exquisite care because Dolben admitted in a letter to Newman, "I owe much to you," and went on to explain how much Newman's novel *Loss and Gain* (a story about conversion) had impressed him. The reason Dolben put off his conversion was that Newman advised him not to be "hasty." Dolben wrote to him:

> I need say nothing about the terrible distress the news of my intention has given at my home—My father and mother seem unable to believe that I am in earnest—and what they say of the presumption of taking such a step at my age, I cannot of course answer satisfactorily to them. When I think of them and of all the dear friends I grieve, I can only repeat over & over the words of yr. letter, "God who has called me will carry me through."[6]

My heart goes out to the nineteen-year-old. He understood that his conversion would alienate him from his family and his friends. Hopkins faced a similar predicament. He too lost friends and became a "stranger" to his family, a high price to pay for one's beliefs. But both of these young men were in earnest: they were not the victims of a sentimental yearning; rather, they believed that the Roman Catholic Church was the *true* Church; thus, they were willing to sacrifice *everything* to ensure the salvation of their souls.

Dolben took his entrance examination for Balliol on May 2, 1867, but fainted and had to leave. Balliol was Hopkins' college, and it was

Robert Bridges who introduced the two, hoping that Hopkins would clue his cousin in about life there and even perhaps help him to win entrance into the highly esteemed college.

Dolben and Hopkins shared many similar interests. Both admired Newman, having read his novel *Loss and Gain*. Both admired Henry Liddon, who had been in charge of the Anglican parish of Finedon, where Dolben lived. Both young men had had their poems published in the *Union Review*. When they met, both were Tractarian in belief, and both were devoted to the Virgin Mary. Both had pushed their Anglicanism to the limits; although neither had yet decided to convert, they surely supported each other in discussing "going over" to Rome. They also shared their poems with each other.

One would assume that the groundwork was perfect for a close friendship to develop between Dolben and Hopkins. As it happened, however, the two never met again. Dolben died a tragically early death, and in the intervening time he never answered the letters that Hopkins sent him. These unanswered letters must have pained Hopkins much; there is an echo of it in one of the Terrible Sonnets composed in Dublin: "And my lament / Is like cries countless, cries like dead letters sent / To dearest him that lives alas! away."

Dolben's tragic, early death came about when he was teaching Walter Prichard, the young son of his tutor, to swim. They had swum across a deep pool with Walter on Dolben's back. On the furthest bank they stood briefly, and then Dolben said he would swim back with Walter. Walter asked Dolben if he were tired. Dolben dismissed the notion but then seemingly had a cramp while swimming, and he and Walter sank into the water. Walter felt Dolben's hands holding him up, and he took the cue to float on his back. Dolben's head, however, never emerged from the water. Walter shouted until help arrived, but Dolben's body had disappeared and was only found

46

hours later. Forty years after the incident, Walter Prichard said simply that Dolben drowned trying to save him.

One would expect to find in Hopkins' journal many entries about the death of Dolben, but there are few. Hopkins' journals rarely reflected his true feelings (the typical British stiff-upper-lip mask was one Hopkins wore). It was in a letter to Robert Bridges that we learn something of what Hopkins felt when he learned of the death of his friend. He said that he found it

> difficult to realize his death [had occurred] or feel as if it were anything to me. You know there can very seldom have happened the loss of so much beauty (in body and mind and life) and of the promise of still more as there has been in his case....Some day I hope to see Finedon and the place where he was drowned too.[7]

Hopkins and Dolben spent only a few days together, but those days had a lasting impact on Hopkins. Robert Bernard Martin, one of Hopkins' biographers, devotes two chapters to Dolben, suggesting that their meeting is the key to the Terrible Sonnets. His poem about Dolben, "Where art thou friend, whom I shall never see, / Conceiving whom I must conceive amiss?" was not included in Bridges' first collection of Hopkins' poems, but it has appeared in the standard collections since then, such as the *Poems of Gerard Manley Hopkins*, edited by W. H. Gardner and N. H. Mackenzie.

I've been thinking about both Dolben and Hopkins and the influence of Newman's novel *Loss and Gain* on both of them. I remember as a young man taking the book out of the library, and I know I started the book, but did I finish it?

Ah, I now remember. The subtitle of the book is *The Story of a Convert*. The main character is Charles Reding, who in the end converts to Rome, but because he does, he is denied his Oxford degree—which nearly happened to Hopkins.

I don't know if many people today read Newman's autobiographical novel. I know his actual autobiography, his *Apologia Pro Vita Sua*, is still popular. I still have my leather-bound copy bought many years ago from my bookseller who sold only finely made books.

I have my Newman's *Apologia* before me now. It's the Oxford Edition, published in 1913. To the right of the title page is a fine copy of a portrait of a young Newman drawn by W. Richmond, now owned by England's National Portrait Gallery. My copy has a rather long Introduction by Wilfrid Ward. In his first paragraph, he writes:

> The public rightly regards the *Apologia* as the most typical and important of the writings of its author. In the first place, it is, in some ways, his most characteristic work. It is instinct with his personality. It is the best exhibition in Newman's published writings of his curious absorption in the drama of his own life. It illustrates the gifts which his greatest enemies have not denied him—his "regal" English style, and his mastery of the methods of effective controversy.[8]

For people to understand Hopkins' conversion, I say they must read Newman's *Apologia*. It's likely the one book that most influenced Hopkins to convert. It's not easy reading. I remember a former student who had written his term paper on Newman. He nearly gave up because the Victorian prose was too florid for him, and the juggling of theological ideas overwhelmed him. I had warned him that it was a difficult book, and when I agreed to let him change to another author (it was his junior year, when we concentrate on British literature), he declined and plowed on. If I remember correctly, he received an honor grade for his efforts.

Hopkins' spiritual mentor, beatified by Pope Benedict XVI in September 2010, is now on the road to canonization. Before Newman's beatification, there was much controversy about disinterring his body from its final resting place. Newman was quite clear and insistent about his being buried with his longtime friend Ambrose St. John: "I wish with all my heart, to be buried in Fr. Ambrose St. John's grave—and I give this as my last, my imperative will." He ended, "This I confirm and insist on." In expressing this wish, Newman knew he would also be resting alongside the graves of his fellow Oratorians Frs. Joseph Gordon and Edward Caswall as well, both of whom had sacrificed much to build up the Oratory. Newman wished to be buried among his Oratorian brothers, perhaps as a reminder that saints do not become saints on their own, and as the end of his life approached, he drew up an illustration of the graves under a cruciform plan.

The Church authorities, however, wanted Newman reburied in the Oratory church in Birmingham, as befits an individual declared "blessed," but when they opened up the grave, they discovered that Newman's casket had been wooden and because the ground was so damp, there wasn't much left. There'll be no relics from that gravesite!

Newman will become the first English saint for forty years. In September 2010 Pope Benedict XVI declared him "Blessed"—the next stage on the path to sainthood. One miracle has already been attributed to the late cardinal (a miracle reported in Massachusetts). He will need a second to become a saint.

Which makes me wonder: Is there a chance that Hopkins may someday be declared a saint? From all that I've read about him, I'd say he is certainly worthy of consideration.

By today's standards of canonization, I wonder if even Augustine would have passed the Church's litmus test. Augustine knew well the bordellos of Carthage, and for a time he lived in a relationship with a concubine and fathered a child out of wedlock, a son whom he named Adeodatus, meaning "gift from God." How fortunate he was to have a mother to pray for his salvation. And then later the honor of being declared a saint! So who knows, maybe there's hope for Hopkins.

The path to sainthood doesn't imply a life lived free of imperfections. Far from it! Take Thomas Merton and his brief romance with a nurse when he was a monk (see Merton's own account in his unexpurgated journal, *Learning to Love*). And Dorothy Day with a child out of wedlock. Oh, well, enough said, but this doesn't stop me from considering Hopkins, Merton, Nouwen, and Day as saints. And I'm not alone, for many people venerate and emulate them. Many Catholics already consider John Paul II a saint, and many are inspired to follow his holy example, especially in regard to physical suffering, for he was a man who courageously carried his cross of suffering.

Hopkins also carried his cross: He was frail and suffered from a number of physical ailments, but he never allowed them to interfere with his duties as a Jesuit. Even his frustrations and disappointments and the resulting bouts of depression, didn't stop him from fulfilling his vocational demands (as a priest, that is).

His Oxford friends were kind when it came to Hopkins' physical frailty. On a walking tour in the summer of 1866, Hopkins' companion William Addis quietly tried to make the walking as easy as possible for him. They visited Tintern Abbey and later went on to Belmont and the Benedictine Cathedral Priory of St. Michael. It was here that Hopkins talked for the first time with a Catholic priest. The topic of discussion was the doubtful validity of Anglican orders. Addis said many years later, "And I believe from that time our faith in Anglicanism was really gone."[9] Yet Hopkins still continued communicating in the Church of England even after he had decided to embrace Rome.

That summer he was much distracted by his spiritual dilemma, about how to inform his family and friends that he was about to abandon the Church of England. He was unable to study, and he was often rude to his friends, not showing up for teas and not preparing them when it was his turn. On July 17, he wrote in his journal:

Dull, curds-and-whey-clouds faintly at times—It was this night I believe but possibly the next that I saw clearly the impossibility of staying in the Church of England, but resolved to say nothing to anyone till three months are over, that is the end of the Long, and then of course to take no step till after my Degree.[10]

Hopkins, likely remembering what had happened to Charles Reding in Newman's *Loss and Gain*, had to keep his intended conversion a secret until he had won his degree. He was, however, bursting to share his decision with some of his intimates, which he did and later regretted. He also shared his secret with his brother Arthur, or, rather, Arthur "forced it from me by questions."[11]

Hopkins decided he had to seek Newman's advice, as had Digby Dolben. In fact, they had both headed for Newman's Oratory at the same time and just missed each other. Newman was absent from the Oratory when Dolben arrived, barefoot, wearing his monk's habit, but his former Eton master J. T. Walford happened to be there. Walford later wrote:

I was in the chapel of Our Lady in the church of the Oratory praying for the conversion of my Eton friends, when the Sacristan called me to the parlour. There I beheld Dolben, whom I had not seen since his Eton days. Eton! What would it have thought of him now!—he was in such a state—bareheaded, muddy and torn. He was wearing the habit of the Anglican Order, he had been hooted in the streets, mud had been thrown at him, he must have been pelted, in short, I don't know how he came to be in such a state. But his face was radiant, I can never forget it. It shone with joy and peace and seemed to light up the room. He said little of his adventure, but that he had come to consult Newman. Newman was away, but I hastened to call Father Ryder.[12]

As I said earlier, Newman did write to Dolben, addressing the young man's anxiety about going against his father's wishes. Newman counseled him to forestall his conversion until he was of age or until his father consented. It was sound advice, for the young man had no means of supporting himself and could have found himself homeless. Newman ended his letter, "In the meanwhile I look on you as one of us."[13] To be treated so beautifully by this man of legend, well, Dolben must have been blissful when he received Newman's letter.

Hopkins had more luck. He met the great man. Ever since Hopkins had arrived at Oxford, he modeled himself after Newman, a legendary man whose charisma and oratorical skills were still talked about at Oxford. Newman had been in virtual seclusion since his own conversion in 1845. Hopkins' biographer Robert Bernard Martin says that, when Hopkins finally met him, he was charmed by Newman, who laughed easily and who was casual and even slangy in his speech, which was the antithesis of his elegant prose.

Newman saw no reasons against Hopkins' being at once received into the Church, but he did advise him to attend a Christmas retreat before his reception; he also suggested that it would be best for him first to finish his degree at Oxford. In no way had Newman tried to rush Hopkins into the Church. His advice was sound and wise.

But Hopkins had his own ideas. He was adamant about being received into the Church as quickly as possible. His parents were vacationing in France at the time of his final decision. He wrote to them rather than tell them face-to-face. He knew his parents would do everything they could to dissuade him from becoming a Catholic, and by letter they employed every argument. But Hopkins showed his mettle: he would not budge from his decision.

Some people have criticized him for being insensitive to his parents at this time, saying that he should have at least told them in person. But I believe Hopkins was wise to inform him the way he did: it was less stress on him and on his parents. For surely, if he had gone home to Hampstead to break the news, he would have been on intolerant ground: his family possessed a repugnance for Catholics as strong as that of Hopkins' friend Robert Bridges. Why should he have submitted himself to that? He was of age, and he needed no one's approval. And he truly believed his immortal soul was at stake; thus, the sooner he was received into the sacred embrace of the one, true, Roman Catholic Church, the better for him.

Today I received a lovely letter from Father Bill McNichols, the famous iconographer. He has finally agreed to my commission for an icon of Gerard Manley Hopkins. He has already done an icon of the poet, for he too admires his fellow Jesuit. I want an icon to commemorate the publication of my Hopkins novella, *The Secret Dublin Diary of Gerard Manley Hopkins.* I am delighted he has agreed to do it. It will take time because Father Bill throws himself into the "writing" of an icon by praying, fasting, and studying the life of the subject.

Father Bill sent me some of his own poetry. I was thrilled to find a poem inspired by Hopkins. It reads:

February 6th

There must be
more than a touch
of Hopkins
in the air,
for everything now
is transparent
and all that is
seen and unseen
reminds me of
You.
The slightest movement
the nod of a tree
the flutter of city
spattered birds,

the cast of shadows
of cobalt blue
on the pavement
And the people
Whose shells evoke
love.
I am all gratitude
spilling over
like the Seven Falls,
a warm flow of tears
simply
from having felt Your
love
again inside
this afternoon.[14]

What a beautiful poem! As lovely as Marie Ponsot's poem titled "Thank Gerard."

I'd like to call Hopkins Gerry, but I understand his actual nickname was Skins, a reference to his surname. But in its own way, it's an appropriate name, for Hopkins seemed to be an exquisite feeler of the world. The world seemed to seep through all his senses—with the "skin" of his senses so sensitively thin that he took in more of the world than most of us. Which is one reason why we need poets: they help us raise our consciousness, help us appreciate the beauty, as Father Bill's poem suggests, of a simple afternoon.

I know I'm grateful for poets. Otherwise, I think I may have sleep-walked through life. But because I've always loved poetry, I've been the recipient of their constant admonition: "Wake up and look!"

When I read Jay Parini's lovely, brief book *Poetry Matters*, I winced at the opening paragraph:

> Poetry doesn't matter to most people. That is, most people don't write it, don't read it, and don't have any idea why anybody would spend valuable time doing such a thing.[15]

Although I'm reluctant to say it, he's right. When it came time for me to teach poetry, my students would literally groan. They hated poetry. I'm not sure of the reasons behind their loathing, but one of them is surely related to the intellectual effort that some poetry demands in order to be understood. One cannot be passive when reading poetry. Reading poetry requires one's undivided attention. The reader must give himself over completely to a close reading, necessitating a self-forgetting at which most people balk or even resent.

But usually, on the positive side, I would, by the end of my poetry unit, win a few students over to liking poetry. In fact, I remember one young woman who shyly remained after class to speak with me. She held in her hand a notebook, which she handed to me, saying that she'd written some poems. Would I read them and let her know "if they were any good"? I read them, and they were quite good.

Many years later I ran into her parents at church, and I asked them about their daughter. She had graduated from college, was married with two children. I was pleased to hear all this information, and they informed me that their daughter had become a writer. My heart leapt, for I immediately thought, "Oh, she's a poet!" Their daughter had just published her first book, a collection of short stories. I admit I was a bit disappointed, but short stories and poems, well, it's close enough.

On October 20, 1866, Hopkins wrote to his mother that his decision to become a Roman Catholic was "irrevocable." The next day he traveled to the Oratory in Birmingham and was received into the Church by Newman. His mother received his letter two days later in Hampstead.

Hopkins had achieved his goal. Although his family had vehemently fought against his becoming a Catholic, they did not ostracize him. Hopkins had feared that his father would never allow him again into his home, but he didn't. Hopkins always remained a beloved member of his family. His little brother Lionel, who was twelve at the time, couldn't understand what all the fuss was about.

For Hopkins, his conversion was an important rite of passage: he had done something quite brave for an Englishman, and he proved to all who knew him that he was his own man (Manley). No one could tell him what to do: not his father, not his mother, not Newman, not his teachers, and surely not his friends. He knew there would be a price to pay, and he did lose some of his friends and the good will of some of his tutors, whom he highly respected. A high price, but one he was willing to pay for his convictions, especially when they concerned his immortal soul.

Now a Catholic, he had to choose what he would *do* in life. He began to think of a religious vocation.

From 1868 to 1874, Hopkins wrote very little poetry. There are fragments, but no complete poems. He narrowed his selection of religious orders down to two: the Benedictines and the Society of Jesus, the Jesuits. In the end he chose the Jesuits. He was attracted by the rigor of their Rule; he was also aware that they were well known as a highly intellectual order. Even Newman praised his choice, saying that the Jesuits would lead him to heaven.

Hopkins lived at the Jesuit seminary Manresa House from 1868 to 1870. It was located at Roehampton, a country village not far from their former seminary at Hyde Park Corner (which Dolben had visited, for which he was expelled from Eton).

New to Manresa, Hopkins first had to learn the aspects of the Rule of the Order. And before he could be accepted as a novice, he was required to enter what is known as the "Long Retreat," which is based on St. Ignatius's *Spiritual Exercises* and which lasts thirty days.

At first, he was given a private room but was soon transferred to a dormitory, where he had a small cubicle without a door, only a curtain. Inside the cubicle was a bed, washstand, and pitcher; outside the cubicle stood a small desk. Of course, there was no central heating. The whole effect was spartan, to say the least. And because these young men were being trained to become soldiers for Christ, the harder the training and the severer the conditions, the better. Manresa was essentially a religious boot camp for potential Jesuits, and its rigor must have been a shock to a young man of such exquisite refinement as Hopkins.

After the Long Retreat, Hopkins was given a Jesuit cassock. It was a previously worn cassock; they were often threadbare from use, had turned a patina-like green, and usually didn't fit the recipient. Another asceticism! For the fastidious Hopkins, it must have been another penance, but because he had embraced the Jesuit motto, "For the Greater Glory of God," he, like a good soldier, repressed any distaste and wore his cassock as a badge of honor.

I've already mentioned the ascetic practice of custody of the eyes. Hopkins often subjected himself to it. At Manresa House, from January to July he looked downward most of the time, depriving himself of the beauty of the sky and of Manresa's gardens and parks (it possessed forty-two lush acres of land). To modern people this all appears to be much too extreme, but in the nineteenth century, these practices were common and were gladly done with full will and acceptance because such penance was an offering to God, meant to please him.

Being a poet, it must have been agonizing for a person of such rare sensibilities to sacrifice beholding beauty. That Hopkins faithfully practiced custody of the eyes tells us of the mettle of which he was made; physically fragile, he was actually more like a steel butterfly, appearing delicate but made of hard steel. Yet we know he was not indomitable, but a very vulnerable person after all.

Which makes his Terrible Sonnets all the more intriguing, for what was it that brought him to his knees, not so much in prayerful adoration but in enigmatic defeat?

Hopkins maintained a log of particulars (he described his notebooks as a "treasury of explored beauty"); it returned me to Duns Scotus (1265—1308), whom Hopkins discovered at St. Mary's Stonyhurst, the second Jesuit seminary he attended. Scotus' philosophy was perfectly congruent with Hopkins' philosophy: all creation, down to its tiniest particulars, is imbued with God's presence. Before he had ever read Scotus, Hopkins intuitively understood this idea, culminating in his concepts of *inscape* and *instress.*

Scotus believed that in each particular thing of nature one can discern the "principle of individuation" or what he calls *haecceitas*: the *thisness* or *isness* of a thing. When one becomes aware of the unique nature of a thing—for instance, when one perceives the "treeness" of a particular tree—then one is also simultaneously aware of its creator: God. Thus, all things, divinely sparked because of their Creator, are endowed with significance. Both Scotus and Hopkins rejected the notion of a thing being merely symbolic of God. I'm reminded of Flannery O'Connor's retort to the suggestion that the Holy Eucharist was only symbolic of the Body and Blood of Christ; if it were, she is reported to have said, "Then the hell with it."

The words of Hopkins' verse are also charged with divinity; thus, words too assume greater significance, for each word is a unique thing. His journals are filled with words that fascinated him, and he searched their derivation in order to master their nuanced meanings, later employing them in his poems.

For Hopkins, to look at something intensely offered him a release from the self: he became "unselved" (Hopkins' word). It is similar to what Simone Weil says: "Absolutely unmixed attention is prayer."[16] True prayer demands self-forgetting; thus, in an act of pure attention one becomes "unselved." Although he might have argued the point, Hopkins was in effect praying each time he offered his "unmixed attention" to a particular beauty.

I came across this remarkable passage in Martin's riveting biography of Hopkins:

For Hopkins, to study anything in nature was to bring his full attention to it, breaking down all possible physical, mental or emotional barriers of understanding, so that he seemed to merge with what he was studying. This attention is the source of his striking statement, made at Stonyhurst, of the two-way flow of perception between observer and observed: "What you look hard at seems to look hard at you." In that remark is encapsulated all the openness, receptivity, even generosity, he brought to the observation of what he loved, both for its own sake and for its reflections.[17]

Martin's passage reminds me of a comment by D. H. Lawrence: that poetry is the result of a pure act of attention, demanding a casting away of the umbrella and standing "naked for the fire of Almighty God to go through one."[18]

There is a paradox in Hopkins' (and Scotus') philosophy: to be an individual is our reason for being; yet we are also "created to praise," and we can only do so when we forget our individuality: Hopkins' *unselving*. Each person's praise, therefore, becomes unlike any other's praise, arising from the uniqueness of the individual, who in order to sing God's praise is paradoxically required to self-forget.

Just finished reading an essay on the poet Elizabeth Bishop. She's considered one of America's finest twentieth-century poets. I've tried time and time again to warm to her, but she still leaves me cold.

She reportedly said that she was "object struck." As with Hopkins, she closely observes things, and although her poems are well crafted, precise in their description, and fraught with detail, there is no joy: she comes across as analytical and anatomical, as if her looking is simply done to pass the time. With Hopkins it is quite different; he too is precise and analytical, but his eyes seek to marvel in not merely the external particulars but the glory within them. One imagines that with Hopkins every thing is enveloped by a halo, echoing Blake's comment, "Every thing that lives is holy."

Bishop's poem "One Art" remains one of my favorites, however, but it is unlike most of her poems in that it's not concentrated upon a thing but upon an idea—a wise, magical poem.

At Stonyhurst, Hopkins began truly to feel like a Jesuit. He gave his first sermons there, and they were well received (later, though, his sermons would often seem bizarre because of his use of far-fetched metaphors). But, again, the high point for him at Stonyhurst was his discovery of Duns Scotus, who would remain his favorite theologian for the rest of his life.

Martin's biography of Hopkins offers a thoughtful and well-balanced summary of his life as a Jesuit at the end of the chapter "Stonyhurst":

> The [Jesuit] Order was strict, but it was also solid, and Hopkins needed a firm structure of belief and behaviour within which to move: Newman had known what he was talking about when he said that it was the right spot for him. Even if the Jesuits, like almost everyone else who knew him, failed to recognize his rare quality, they were very kind to him and constantly put up with his awkward but lovable personality. One might ask where Hopkins would have been happier.[19]

I find Martin's last sentence intriguing. Would Hopkins have been happier in another religious order? This question has intrigued not only me but many other people, including a number of Hopkins scholars. For instance, what would his life have been like had he joined the Franciscan Order? His personality had more in common with the founder of the Franciscans than with the founder of the Jesuits. I must ponder this more deeply...

His philosophy studies now finished, Hopkins' next step was theology at St. Beuno's College in Wales.

Years at St. Beuno's

Today I succumbed to purchasing Humphry House's *The Journals and Papers of Gerard Manley Hopkins.* I'm so enamored of Hopkins' prose, I must own the book. It was expensive, and unfortunately not a first edition!

Hopkins' prose is as fine as, if not finer, than that of Francis Kilvert (collected in *Kilvert's Diary, 1840—1879,* edited by William Plomer). Kilvert is not well known. He was an English clergyman, a rural curate. His diaries are primarily descriptions of Wales, where he served for most of his short life. Anyone who enjoys nature writing will be thrilled by his descriptions of the Welsh landscape and its people. He saw much suffering among the Welsh and recorded many of the tragic events he encountered during his ministry. His diary, I find, is both beautiful and moving. In the Introduction to *Kilvert's Diary* A. L. Rowse suggests that the greatest diarists of the nineteenth century are Dorothy Wordsworth, Francis Kilvert, and Gerard Manley Hopkins. I own the first two diaries, but the latter I've always taken out on loan from the library. I look forward to its delivery and holding it in my hands.

I never knew anything about Kilvert until I had read the diary of James Schuyler, a Pulitzer Prize poet of the New York School of poetry, which includes such luminaries as Frank O'Hara and John Ashbury; Schuyler records his own delight in reading Kilvert. So I embarked on a book hunt until I finally owned my own copy, which I treasure (my search occurred before the Internet).

The best gift (to myself and to others) is a book.

Kilvert and Hopkins were contemporaries and unknown as writers when alive, only to be discovered in the twentieth century. They were likely touring Wales at the same time, and they both fell in love with the haunting beauty of Wales. They have both secured their place in the pantheon of England's greatest writers, although Hopkins is secure in two genres, in both poetry and prose.

Pivotal dates in Hopkins' seminary life:

1868—70   Manresa House, where he enters Jesuit Novitiate
1870—73   St. Mary's Hall, Stonyhurst, where he discovers
          Duns Scotus
1874—77   St. Beuno's, where he returns to writing poetry

At St. Beuno's College, which is located in a lovely spot overlooking the valley of the Elwy and the Clwyd, Hopkins studied theology. Unfortunately his last extant journal ends in February 1875. It is unlikely that Hopkins stopped keeping a journal, for he was an inveterate diarist. At his death many of his papers were destroyed, including a Dublin journal, for there is one remaining fragment, proving that he had indeed maintained a journal up to the end of his life. What a loss!

The good news, however, is that while at St. Beuno's, Hopkins returned to composing poetry. In 1875, the SS *Deutschland*, a German ship whose passengers included five Franciscan nuns on their way to America, ran aground off the English coast and sank. The event garnered much attention in the English press. Hopkins was very much moved by the news accounts he read, many of which were sent to him by his family (primarily his mother). When the rector of St. Beuno's suggested that a poem be written about the tragic disaster, Hopkins interpreted his comment as a release from his personal "vow" not to write verse and took up the challenge.

At St. Beuno's, Hopkins fell in love not only with the Welsh landscape but also with the Welsh language, and he diligently studied its poetry and complicated metrics. From his studies evolved his own unique rhythm, which he called "sprung rhythm," whose goal is the rhythm of common speech. He was itching to employ it and when he received what he interpreted as the green light to write verse again (although there was no official ban on his composing verse), he responded by writing what many scholars consider his masterpiece: *The Wreck of the Deutschland.*

When I introduced my students to Hopkins' poetry, I never began with this poem because it was far too difficult for them to understand. It takes many readings and much thought to penetrate to the heart of its hidden meaning; most high school pupils, even if they are gifted, as were my students, are daunted by it. Robert Bridges, a highly gifted poet himself, had great difficulty plumbing its meaning. He despairingly compared it to a great dragon at the gate of a cave, forbidding all entry. It's difficult because it was a new kind of poetry, and people tend to be put off by anything new and innovative.

Without his knowing it, Hopkins had actually initiated modern poetry in 1876 when he completed the poem, but it did not see the light of day until 1918, when Bridges published Hopkins' collected poems. Hopkins' own religious order refused to publish *The Wreck* in its magazine *The Month.* It was a terrible blow to Hopkins, because publication would have meant acceptance by his Order, something Hopkins desperately sought: he surely was aware that most of his Jesuit brothers and superiors viewed him as an "eccentric," the word most commonly used by Jesuits to describe Hopkins as a man, as a priest, and as a teacher. After they read his poem about the Deutschland, add "eccentric" as a poet.

In writing *The Wreck of the Deutschland*, Hopkins again fully donned the mantle of poet; he afterward composed some of his best poems, poems studied today in classes all over the world.

I usually introduced my students to Hopkins with either "God's Grandeur" or "Spring and Fall." Bearing the dedication "to a young child," "Spring and Fall" begins: "Márgarét, are you grieving / Over Goldengrove unleaving?" This poem, the antithesis of the opaque *Wreck of the Deutschland*, is both charming and accessible. When Hopkins wrote "Spring and Fall," he was working in a poor parish in Liverpool. The parishioners were plainspoken and uneducated, but they were the souls who had been entrusted to Hopkins' priestly care. And to communicate with them, he had to choose a simpler diction; his lofty Oxford vocabulary and accent wouldn't work in such a setting. Had his choice of a simpler language at that time seeped into his poetic diction?

The poem is written as if Hopkins were actually speaking to a child, and he wasn't talking down to her as we sometimes do with children. He counsels her as a priest is expected to do, offering her spiritual advice, but in order for her to understand, he keeps it simple, or rather, as simple as he can be. To introduce students to Hopkins, it's a good poem to begin with because its message is one a young person can appreciate.

Young people do, indeed, ponder death—as Hopkins said, "the blight man was born for." Some have experienced the loss of parents or other close relatives, and sometimes of friends. At first, students would often find the poem a bit obscure, but with fine-tuned leading questions, they soon discovered the way to the heart of the poem: the young girl is puzzled by the falling leaves because she has yet to understand the concept of death and how it also applies to herself. How gently Hopkins speaks to her, how compassionate his tone of voice, how graciously and reverently he announces her name, "Margaret."

One could easily summarize the poem by stating that, in general, it addresses the loss of innocence. Knowledge of death initiates adult consciousness. Hopkins' direct address to the young girl reveals how he, too, must have reacted to the realization that "death is the mother of beauty," to quote the American poet Wallace Stevens in his poem "Sunday Morning." The young, sensitive Hopkins may also have wept at the sight of falling leaves, the young boy who had often climbed a tree near his house to observe London in the distance. As a young man, Hopkins was fascinated by every kind of tree; his notebook is filled with descriptions of trees. As an adult he actually wept when the Binsey poplars near Oxford were felled in 1879:

My aspens dear, whose airy cages quelled,
Quelled or quenched in leaves the leaping sun,
Áll félled, félled, are áll félled.

How ironic for a young man to advise a girl not to cry, for he himself as an adult could not stop himself from weeping; it illustrates the touching charm of the man, that he could unabashedly weep over the destruction of beauty.

Hopkins' time at St. Beuno's was for the most part happy, although he still suffered from depression and a number of physical ailments. Not only did he glory in the beauty of Wales, and return to writing with *The Wreck of the Deutschland*, but he also composed some of his finest poems: "God's Grandeur," "The Starlight Night," "Spring," "In the Valley of the Elwyn," "The Sea and the Skylark," "The Windhover," "Pied Beauty," "Hurrahing in Harvest," "The Caged Skylark," and "The Lantern Out of Doors."

"The Starlight Night" is a poem whose first lines instantly reminded me of Vincent van Gogh's paintings of the night sky: "Look at the stars! Look, look up at the skies! / O look at all the fire-folk sitting in the air!"

The exclamation marks speak eloquently of Hopkins' joy in the night sky (there are sixteen exclamations in the poem!); he wanted everyone to enjoy the sky, thus the ecstatic cry, "Look!" His poetry is open, not hermetic, and reaches out to his audience; his manner of touching them was both priestly and chaste, the only kind of touch allowed a celibate man.

His poetry seems to say that if you would only look, you would see that the world is indeed charged with the "grandeur of God," and you would perhaps be graced with a glimpse of divinity, an oblique one, but divine nevertheless.

At this moment, I am gazing at a reproduction of Vincent van Gogh's *Starry Night over the Rhone.* It's a glorious painting; he too is sharing his delight in the night sky. Such beauty! Some of Van Gogh's best paintings capture the loveliness of the sky after sunset—and stars were important to him:

> The infinitely distant fires of the pinkish stars, each radiating a complementary green glow against the mysterious, resonant cosmos, were for him not only a manifestation of the same divine energies that governed life on earth, but the signs of

potential abodes for the continuance of artistic lives governed by love and reverence for creation.[1]

"The Starlight Night" suggests that, to enjoy the beauty of the sky, the privilege must be "purchased" through reverence, patience, alms, and vows. The truest down payment, however, is actually rather simple: *pay attention*, or rather, *"Look!"* Creation is God's gift to us: it's gratis for our pleasure and enjoyment, but we must fully use the senses with which God has gifted us.

As an instructor of English literature, I believed that if I could teach my students to pay attention to the beauty of the text at hand, I would also be helping them to observe and to enjoy the beauty of the world. Perhaps mine was an absurd ideal, but in my heart of hearts I believed that what the French call *explication de texte* is vitally important in helping our young people to learn to attend not only to the beauty of a literary work studied in class but also to the beauty of the world. The added value, of even greater importance, is that we also learn to pay attention to one another. Is there a greater lesson than this?

Notice what is involved in the physical action of looking up at the sky at the stars. One must bend back one's neck to lift one's head. Many Christian rituals of worship entail descent rather than ascent: we kneel to pray, we bow our heads, we lower our eyes (consider Hopkins' preferred penance, "custody of the eyes"), and we genuflect. For many religious, the most sacred physical gesture involves lying on the floor in a cruciform shape.

But "The Starlight Night" is a poem exhorting the reader to look up. It's a poem not of descent but of ascent: it is analogous to our striving toward and longing for God, and by so doing, we lift ourselves out of our ego-dominated consciousness.

At St. Beuno's there were times of sadness as well. Hopkins failed his final theological exam because he espoused Duns Scotus' philosophy/theology over that of Thomas Aquinas. Such a failure didn't jeopardize his ordination, but it meant that Hopkins would never be promoted to an important post in the Order or become one of the Order's professors, which was a loss to the Jesuits because intellectually Hopkins was surely an intellectual giant, the equal of one of England's greatest intellectuals, John Henry Newman.

Another sadness: none of Hopkins' family attended his ordination. It must have been heartbreaking for the young man, who very likely enviously observed other newly ordained priests joyfully mixing with their families during the festive luncheon offered after the ceremony. He must have felt not only rejected but also very lonely.

To render his ordination even sadder, now that he was ordained, he would soon have to leave his beloved Wales, which he described as "the true Arcadia of wild beauty."[2]

During my three decades of teaching gifted secondary students, I learned which Hopkins poems were the most accessible. As mentioned, I never tried to teach *The Wreck of the Deutschland*; it's a poem to grapple with in college, although I did have one student who, after reading several of Hopkins' lyrics, read it on his own. We discussed the poem, and I was amazed that he was able to penetrate its multilayered meaning. Years later I received a letter from him in which he informed me that poetry had become his passion. He not only read poetry but also wrote it. I've often wondered if it was Hopkins who inspired him to embark down that particular road.

One of the "simpler" lyrics I presented to my class was "Pied Beauty," which begins, "Glory be to God for dappled things." I love this poem because it reveals how exquisitely attentive Hopkins was to God's world. He truly knew how to behold the world, and I mean *behold* in the sense that Christ meant it when he said, "Behold the lilies of the field": it suggests paying attention to something with one's whole being, so that one actually forgets oneself and enters into a selfless state of being.

Just this week a friend of mine in England sent me an e-mail saying that he now prefers the word *gaze* over *see* because it implies a deeper kind of seeing. I wrote back to him that I myself preferred *behold* because it is the kind of seeing that becomes a part of one's being: one holds onto what one *beholds*, to the point that it becomes a part of one's being.

This is the kind of seeing exemplified in "Pied Beauty." As with the contemporary poet Mary Oliver, Hopkins similarly hoped to be "a bride married to amazement" and a "bridegroom, taking the world into my arms."[3]

Hopkins lived at an exquisite "pitch" of being-ness; *pitch* was one of his favorite words. He gloried in everything he beheld, no matter how humble or miniscule it was; in "Pied Beauty," it was rose-moles on a fish, chestnuts dashed open by falling from a tree, and the wings of a finch—such a small bird. The poem was not blind to the larger beauties either. Anyone who has ever flown over England in an airplane knows full well what Hopkins meant when he described its landscape as "plotted and pieced": rectangular and square plots of land are neatly delineated, some formed for containing sheep, others for declaring boundaries of farmland.

His eyes, which he had tried to discipline through the ascetic practice of custody of the eyes, sought all things that were "counter, original, spare, strange." It's as if Hopkins believed, as does the poet Mary Oliver: "To pay attention, this is our endless and proper work."[4]

My students invariably asked the meaning of the poem's title, "Pied Beauty." I would then read the definition of *pied* from the dictionary: "Patchy, in color; splotched, piebald." Then I'd explain the meaning of each word in the definition because most of the students were unclear as to their meaning. I'd also explain, as they were wont to ask, that *pied* is pronounced not as two syllables but as one, the i a long i.

So from the start with the poem's title, I had plenty to explain. I'd then encourage my students to dive into the poem's meaning, like a swimmer into beckoning water. I'd urge them not to be intimidated by the poem's strange originality (for surely Hopkins was aware that his poems were "counter, original, spare, strange") and simply plunge into the ten-line sonnet. And there would always ensue a debate about whether or not "Pied Beauty" was, indeed, a sonnet, for hadn't I repeatedly taught them that sonnets always contain fourteen lines!

Students, as suggested, must first understand the poem's diction: *brinded, stipple, finch, fold*, and *fallow*. Once the vocabulary was mastered, we were more prepared to delve more deeply into meaning.

Students had no difficulty understanding that Hopkins' poem was a prayer. And unlike the one student who challenged me about religious poetry being taught in a public school, no student ever questioned me about teaching Hopkins' "Pied Beauty" as a poem/prayer.

Few students knew anything about Jesuits, so I would also offer a brief history of the Order of the Society of Jesus, or Jesuits, and related the Order's Latin motto: *Ad Majorem Dei Gloriam*, which my students had no trouble translating as they all had studied Latin, a four-year requirement.

One cannot fully appreciate Hopkins' poem unless one understands this motto. The life of each Jesuit is dedicated to offering glory to God. All of one's life, including every thought and deed, is to be devoted to the greater glory of God—which meant that everything one saw, heard, touched, smelled, and tasted was offered to God, the Source of everything; thus, each Jesuit constantly praises and thanks God for his munificence. And it's exactly what Hopkins accomplishes in this poem: he praises God for everything he sees, no matter how miniscule, even the row of small dots on a fish, whose pattern possesses its own beauty, its own *inscape*, reflective of God's own infinite beauty, power, creativity, and variety.

Ezra Pound said that it is better to present one image in a lifetime than to produce voluminous works.

He suggested that when writing poetry one should use no superfluous word, no adjective that does not reveal something important. For instance, one shouldn't use such an expression as "dim lands of peace." An adjective dulls the image. It mixes an abstraction with the concrete. It comes from the writer's not realizing that the natural object is always the adequate symbol. Drop the word *dim*. Such a way of writing applies to prose too. Hemingway used adjectives sparingly, focusing on the thing itself. In fact, it has become axiomatic in today's writing classes (and how they've proliferated!) to avoid adjectives. Of course, this is extreme, but I myself am a minimalist in my writing, using few adjectives in both my nonfiction and fiction.

I have finished reading the fine new biography *Gerard Manley Hopkins: A Life* by Paul Mariani, who is (as I wrote in my review for amazon.com) "likely our finest, living American biographer of poets...[and] one of our best, close readers of Hopkins' admittedly difficult verse." Mariani is such an admirable man whose intellectual brilliance is matched by only one other of my teachers, Professor

Helen Vendler of Harvard. She is also one of our finest poetry critics. My only reservation about her approach to poetry is that she's too cerebral, whereas Professor Mariani allows feeling a place in his teaching and in his criticism. Since all poetry addresses emotion in some fashion, critics shouldn't be afraid of it.

As a teacher of English literature, I have often used in class Wordsworth's definition of poetry: "emotion recollected in tranquility." Generally speaking, all poetry presents some strong, subjective emotion.

Even an Imagist poet cannot escape emotion: it is revealed in the very thing that has been chosen as subject (or perhaps the object has chosen the poet).

Back to "Pied Beauty": "All things counter, original, spáre, strange" has me thinking. Had Hopkins thought of himself as "strange"? The word derives from the Latin *extraneus*, meaning "outside." Later, in Dublin, in one of his Terrible Sonnets, Hopkins employs the word *stranger* to describe himself. All of this suggests to me that Hopkins was "alien" and thus a terribly lonely man. And when one feels so strange, so alien, there is always someone to turn to: God, although, as we shall learn, God was sometimes silent and distant from Hopkins—but *not* absent. Hopkins' life became dark in its last years, but it was never totally dark, although to some readers it seems that way. More anon.

Ted Kennedy, America's great liberal lion, is dead. Recently it was his sister who died; today it is her brother. I cannot help feeling that an era has come to an end. He chose to have his funeral Mass at Mission Church (now a basilica) in Roxbury, Massachusetts, well known in its heyday for its Wednesday novena to Our Lady of Perpetual Help. As a kid, I remember going to the novena, and there would be buses lined up in front of the church, and inside there would be standing room only. Father Manton, a legendary priest famous as an orator, led the novena. The novena continues to this day, attended by mostly Hispanic Catholics (replacing the earlier Boston Irish). But the number of people has drastically dwindled. Sad.

I remember as an adult going out to dinner with Father Manton, in his nineties at the time. And when he ordered a martini, I liked him the more.

Today, all flagpoles are at half-mast for Ted Kennedy. Although I differed politically from him on many issues, I know that he did much good for the poor and disenfranchised, and I now hear from many pundits that his legacy will be considered far greater than either of his brothers, John and Robert. Perhaps. One thing is certain: Massachusetts has lost its champion, and there is no one of such stature on the horizon to replace him. I shudder to think of some of the people who might seek his senate seat. (Later note: The seat was ultimately lost to a Republican, a seeming slap in the face to the Kennedy clan.)

Today is Thursday, and Ted Kennedy will lie in state at the Kennedy Library here in Boston, starting tonight at 6:00 p.m. His funeral Mass will take place on Saturday at the Basilica of Our Lady of Perpetual Help. I have since learned that he prayed there for his daughter when she was treated for cancer at a nearby hospital. He also prayed there for himself, after discovering he too had cancer.

Many miracles have allegedly occurred at this church. It's been many years since I've been inside, but I still remember the pyramid of canes and crutches that filled a corner of the church, those of sick people who had been cured through their novenas to Our Lady of

Perpetual Help. I remember being moved when I first saw this pyramid of wood. But the church recently underwent extensive renovations, and only a few of the canes and crutches remain. A shame if it's true. Why disband the "relics" of cure? Not decorative enough? Or is belief in miracles passé?

I'm reminded of Hopkins' pilgrimages to St. Winefred's Well in Wales, which is famous for its healing powers. Hopkins himself bathed in the water. He believed the well still possessed its curative powers and noted in his journal how a young man from Liverpool had been healed of a rupture. St. Winefred's cult was first associated with that of St. Beuno, and in its earliest years it was confined to North Wales. Winefred was the daughter of a Welsh chieftain. When she refused to be seduced by another chieftain, he had her beheaded. Where her head fell, a spring burst forth. When Beuno returned her head to her body, she returned to life and lived another fifteen years. Her well and the chapel built around it go back to the seventh century and have continued as a place of pilgrimage to this day.

The well meant more to Hopkins than any other site in Wales because its Catholicism had never been disturbed or interrupted; its well was maintained for centuries by a nearby Cistercian abbey and later secretly cared for by Jesuits. To Hopkins, the pious pilgrimages of countless Catholics to the shrine kept one location of Great Britain true to the Catholic faith, and the fact that Jesuits had an important role in its preservation was important to him. It's no wonder he wrote, in her honor, a brief poem about St. Winefred. He had also written a play about St. Winefred, but as with so many of Hopkins' works, it was never finished.

I meant to spend the day with Hopkins, but I found myself glued to the TV watching Ted Kennedy's funeral. The Mass at the Basilica of Our Lady of Perpetual Help was beautifully celebrated. His two sons delivered heartfelt eulogies; Placido Domingo and Yo Yo Ma offered a duet of *Panis Angelicus*, and Susan Graham of the New York Metropolitan Opera sang Schubert's *Ave Maria*. It was all so exquisitely done, a fitting tribute to a great man.

Afterward the body was flown to the Arlington Cemetery where it was buried near his two brothers, John and Robert. It was haunting to watch the sunset burial service. After the burial, many of the Kennedy family walked over to JFK's eternal flame, and I was very much touched by the sight of all these living Kennedys standing in the night before the flame, all silently gazing. It was all very moving.

When I turned off the TV, I thought: What a poem Hopkins could have written about such an event. He would have captured the setting sun and its crimson sky, the two maple trees flanking Ted's grave, the eerie silence of the crowd that understood something historical was happening before them, and the crowd praying together the prayer Christ taught us, the Our Father. Oh, what a poem he could have composed!

The Wreck of the Deutschland begins: "Thou mastering me / God! Giver of breath and bread."

Where had I just seen this word *master* in Hopkins? Ah, yes, I was impressed by Hopkins' reaction to the windhover's mastery. (Both "The Windhover" and *Deutschland* were written at St. Beuno's.) Why is this concept of mastery so much on the poet's mind? I must explore this a bit more, for what I've previously concluded may indeed be too superficial.

Jesuits are often called the soldiers of Christ. They therefore have a master: God, who "masters" them through the writings of St. Ignatius's *Spiritual Exercises* (a manual for a spiritual boot camp).

Hopkins always admired soldiers. His poem "The Soldier" begins by asking: "Yes. Whý do we áll, seeing of a soldier, bless him? bless / Our redcoats, our tars?"

Soldiers serve under a master. They take orders; they have no right to assert themselves. They must be humble and do everything that they are ordered to do. Such a way of life appealed to Hopkins. He chose the rigorous Jesuits over the less severe Franciscans and Benedictines. It appears that he desired to be formed into one of Christ's soldiers, and to do so he had to surrender himself to be mastered both externally and inwardly.

In the opening of *Deutschland*, God is viewed as supreme master: God is omnipotent, the master of the earth and the cosmos; he is also the cause of the storm and the wreck, and his power is exhibited both by the storm and by its wrecking of the steamship, and because God allowed the wreckage and the seventy-eight deaths, including the five Franciscan nuns, there must be a divine purpose behind the tragedy.

Took a break from Hopkins today to browse through *Stepping Stones: Interviews with Seamus Heaney* by Dennis O'Driscoll. I've always admired Seamus Heaney's poems and had the good fortune to meet him twice. Heaney says that the two poets that most influenced him when he was young were Robert Frost and Gerard Manley Hopkins. Of the latter he says that by the third year at Queen's University, he was a "slave to Hopkins."[5] I wasn't surprised that Hopkins influenced him.

When Heaney attended St. Columb's, his Catholic formation wasn't much different from Hopkins. He says, "What you encounter in Hopkins' journals—the claustrophobia and scrupulosity and religious ordering of the mind, the cold-water shaves and the single iron beds, the soutanes and the self-denial—that was the world I was living in when I first read his poems."[6]

I've just completed a rereading of *The Wreck of the Deutschland*. No doubt about it: it's as compelling and complex as a Bach fugue. One must completely hand oneself over to it; otherwise, one will never penetrate its multilayered meanings. I've used Norman H. Mackenzie's *Reader's Guide* to help guide me through this stirring ode. It's stirring because it contains all of Hopkins' hopes, desires (past, present, and future), skill in language, and, generally, poetic genius, offering to us a new kind of poetry, one no one had ever before written.

The word *master* and its variations are used eight times in the poem, and when he capitalizes *master*, he is specifically referring to Christ. Hopkins is stirred by the power and majesty of the storm because it allows him to be mastered by the "Lord of living and dead."

Today is the first day of autumn. It's been an unpredictable day of gray skies and a peeping sun. Currently there's no sunlight.

I'm in the midst of a second reading of scholarly studies of Hopkins' verse and life, and their comments on *The Wreck of the Deutschland* have helped me enormously to understand this most difficult poem. After a careful, close reading of a poem that has for years frightened me by its length, its obscurity, and its distorted diction, I've won new insights.

The Wreck addresses life's greatest mystery: human suffering. Or rather, it addresses the "why?" of so much suffering, especially that of the innocent and the weak.

The bare facts of the poem are these: The German-owned vessel, the *Deutschland*, sailed from Bremerhaven on December 4, 1875, bound for New York. It carried 123 passengers and between ninety and one hundred crewmen. It ran aground on the Kentish Knock of England, a sandbank twenty-five miles south of Harwich, near the mouth of the Thames. Help was very slow in coming. Seventy-eight people died, including five Franciscan nuns who had been banished from Germany by the anti-Catholic Falk Laws enacted as part of Germany's *Kuilturkampf* (cultural war) in 1873.

To a man of faith like Hopkins, the shipwreck was a manifestation of God's omnipotence; he also saw it as an exemplum of suffering similar to the suffering of Jesus, his passion and death. Thus, the heroic deaths of the nuns are not tragic for Hopkins, for the nuns, *in imitatio Christi*, embraced their deaths as God's will for them at that moment in their lives.

The story of the wreck of the *Deutschland*, as a human tragedy, was carried in all the leading English papers. There was much outrage that rescue efforts for the victims were so late and slow arriving. Many of the newspapers noted the story of the tall nun who thrust her body through the ship's sky light, exclaiming, "O Christ, Christ, come quickly."

Hopkins not only considered the nun heroic, but victorious over intense suffering by submitting herself to God, calling upon him as she would call upon a lover (as a nun, she is a bride of Christ). By rejecting abnegation and fear, she transcended an ignoble disaster with its suffering and death.

I'm still reading Jay Parini's *Why Poetry Matters*. I was particularly pleased to read the following: "I myself consider poetry a form of religious as well as political thought. A poem, for me, is an integration....In the end, it brings us closer to God, however we define the term. It provides, in some cases, a reason for life itself."[7]

I have often turned to verse, by poets such as Hopkins, for spiritual nourishment. In fact, I shudder to consider what my life would've been like without the consolations of poetry.

It is important to note that the word *wreck* that Hopkins employed to describe the *Deutschland* not only describes the storm tragedy, but might also have been intended to describe his life before becoming a Catholic. By converting to Catholicism, Hopkins felt that he had finally found a safe harbor, a feeling shared by John Henry Newman, who also felt that by becoming a Catholic he had sailed "into safe port."

There's a famous comment by Ruskin (famous, and yet I can't place my hands on the source!) that I had written down:

> Nothing must come between Nature and the artist's sight; nothing between God and the artist's soul. Neither calculation nor hearsay, —be it the most subtle of calculations, or the wisest of sayings, —may be allowed to come between the universe, and the witness which art bears to its visible nature. The whole value of that witness depends on its being eye-witness; the whole genuineness, acceptableness, and dominion of it depend on the personal assurance of the man who utters it. All its victory depends on the veracity of the one preceding word, "Vidi."

Hopkins read Ruskin's book *Elements of Drawing* at a young age. Ruskin exhorted the artist toward a close observation of nature, to the point that the "selfhood" of the object is of utter importance. Thus, an object's *details* must be noticed and captured, and if one reads Hopkins' journals, one can't help being impressed by his detailed prose descriptions of nature, as well as by his small, precise drawings of landscape or of single aspects of nature like a tree or even a skyscape. It's interesting to note that Hopkins came to Ruskin long before he read Scotus. And Hopkins had coined the words *inscape* and *instress* as early as 1868, before he had discovered Scotus at Stonyhurst and seven years before he wrote *The Wreck of the Deutschland.*

Noticed for the first time a line from *The Wreck* confirming Ruskin's influence on Hopkins. It is from the twenty-ninth stanza: "Ah! there was a heart right! / There was single eye!"

"There was single eye!": here is the heart of the poem. The nun has eyes for one thing: Jesus Christ. For a long time as a Franciscan nun, by devotion to Christ through prayer and reading of the scriptures, she has nurtured this "single eye," the very eye that Christ describes as the "lamp of the body" (Matt 6:22).

Hopkins as a Jesuit was also involved in a similar training of the "single eye," but at the same time, he was disciplining himself as a poet, as one who followed Ruskin's advice to observe closely the world around him. His eyes were like microscopes, missing nothing, not the tiniest flower (bluebells, for instance) or the cracks of ice formed in puddles on the ground, with their infinite variations of design; and his eyes could also be telescopic when they horizontally scanned the landscape, with its undulating meadows and moors, and lifted vertically to the English skyscape with its constantly changing plumes, sheets, and pillows of cloud.

My recently deceased friend Dorothy Judd Hall was a Robert Frost scholar who taught at Boston University and lectured at Boston College. She had a great love for BC and for Jesuit priests. She had once gifted me with a book (*Seeing into the Life of Things: Essays on Religion and Literature*, edited by John L. Mahoney, SJ) that contained her own essay on Wallace Stevens.

I vaguely remembered that it contained an essay about Hopkins and after a long search for it (I'm not organized when it comes to books, which are scattered throughout my home), I found it and realized why these two lines about the "single eye" leapt out at me, for J. Robert Barth, SJ, caught the importance of the image in his essay, "The Sacramental Vision of Gerard Manley Hopkins." He writes:

In order to achieve this perception—of God and his creation in a single act of vision—one must have what Hopkins calls a "single eye." The phrase is from "The Wreck of the Deutschland," where it is attributed to the tall nun, the leader of the five Franciscan nuns who went to their death on the fateful night of December 7, 1875. In the midst of terror and suffering, of darkness and confusion, she found Christ, calling out to him: "O Christ, Christ, come quickly."[8]

As a teacher of English, I tried to help my students become one with the text, which requires a self-forgetting; to understand a poem, for instance, they need silence so that they can offer their complete attention to the text, for only in silence can one become one with the text. It's the only way to read poetry: with the single eye of unmixed attention.

As an analogy, Hopkins read the world with his "single eye," for the whole world, the cosmos even, is the Word of God, or rather, God's text. Therefore, one has to expand one's "lexicon" by intently gazing at the objects of the world: its trees, its stones, its flowers, its sky, its snow, its rain, its ice, its leaves, its roots, etc. And if one does this, one is actually observing, to use St. Bonaventure's term, "vestiges" of divinity (*The Soul's Journey into God*), All things God has created; thus, all things reflect God's presence. Therefore, a tree is a "word" of God. But each tree is a different "word," for Hopkins believed in the *inscape* of every tree: each one is different in a unique way from every other tree.

An aesthetic (and theological) perspective like that of Hopkins appealed to modern poets, particularly the early twentieth-century Imagists like Ezra Pound, Hilda Doolittle, William Carlos Williams, and Amy Lowell. The Imagist poetic revolution, a modernist Anglo-American movement spearheaded by Ezra Pound, produced verse that allows the images to speak for themselves. Imagist verse was influenced by Oriental poetry such as the haiku and the tanka, poems strictly limited by the number of lines and syllables. The emphasis in these poems was not in ideas but in things—or rather, one thing.

St. Beuno's College had a stuffed bird in a cage, part of the Waterton Collection. A caption identified the bird as a kestrel, or windhover. Yet it was surely his close observation of the living bird hovering/flying in the air that must have fired Hopkins' imagination for the poem.

After reading it several times, I wondered what it was that so captured his attention (and imagination), what attributes he had seen in the bird but not in himself. And for me at least, the lines "My heart in hiding / Stirred for a bird, —the achieve of; the mastery of the thing!" summarizes the meaning of the poem.

His heart stirred for a bird because the bird was the master of its own life, of its own actions, of its own being. To Hopkins this was the supreme achievement: the bird is freely itself, and beautifully.

Notice Hopkins' use of the word *thing*. He was, again, definitely the precursor of Ezra Pound, for Pound advised poets to zero in on "the thing itself." The result is a minimalist poetry that is very like Japanese poetry, similar, for example, to the haiku, but Imagist poems are usually longer than the haiku's seventeen syllables. William

Carlos Williams' "The Red Wheelbarrow," with its twenty-one syllables, is perhaps our most famous American Imagist poem.

I see in my mind's eye Hopkins' watching the windhover maneuvering in the sky (I'm employing Ignatius's imaginative "composition of place"). Hopkins was a sky-watcher. As mentioned, one need only browse for a few pages into his journals to find descriptions of sky-scapes. But in this case it's not so much the sky as it was the bird and how it maneuvered in the sky with its constantly shifting air currents.

Watching the bird circling in the sky, Hopkins exclaimed, "In his ecstasy!" Here is a fine example of what's known as "pathetic fallacy," or the attribution of human characteristics to an inanimate object or to nature: the bird is not ecstatic, it was Hopkins himself who was. Hopkins was an eye-ecstatic, by which I mean he was exquisitely attentive to the beauty of the world, seeing it everywhere, and at its sight he often experienced ecstasy. But for Hopkins, seeing beauty was not merely an aesthetic experience; it was also a spiritual one, for all beauty reminded him of God; thus the poem's dedication, "To Christ our Lord."

Hopkins transformed the bird into an emblem of Christ; the poem exclaims Christ's omnipresent beauty; therefore, the windhover was also for Hopkins a symbol of divine beauty and mastery, far greater than the "billion times" loveliness of the bird itself.

Critics have tried to nail down the meaning of the word *buckle* in the second stanza. What does Hopkins mean by it? It must, I feel, refer to some movement of the bird. Does it perform an unexpected motion? Does it turn, bend, warp, or crumple in an unusual manner (buckle) to the point that its suddenness and beauty make Hopkins' knees buckle (bend a common definition)?

The last stanza exhibits a shift of gaze. The poet is now looking not at the sky dominated by the windhover but at the earth. The earth too possesses its own beauty: he describes the wonder of it with its ploughed dirt shining in the sun, its gutted ploughs reminding him of the gash in the side of Christ's body on the cross. For the earth to give forth the food we need to live, it is "wounded" by a sharp plough. Christ too had to be wounded (by nails and a lance) to die in order to save us (and for us to have life more abundantly, John 10:10) by his suffering, death, and resurrection. The shift of attention from the bird to Christ's crucifixion is a swift one. The reader doesn't expect it, but neither does the poet expect the quickness (quick also as life) of the windhover's flight or sky maneuvering: an incredibly unpredictable and dazzling-to-behold "dance" in the sky (although the poet compares the bird's motion to riding a horse), one so majestic the poet can only think in royal terms: "daylight's dauphin."

"The Windhover" is such a rich poem. But with my new reading, I have achieved insights that I hope will lead to more insights. But I am still perplexed by a single phrase, "My heart in hiding." I again ask, "Hiding from what?" Surely the bird wouldn't fly away because of the poet's watching it. And it certainly wouldn't attack him: there was simply no danger involved. Yet I feel the key to the poem lies in this phrase, and I know I must ponder it more deeply.

Perhaps the hiding has something to do with masks. I'm still reading Jay Parini's *Why Poetry Matters*; in his chapter on Yeats he addresses Yeats's concept of the mask, which derives from the Latin word *persona*. Parini writes, "In all writing, the author must self-authorize: create his or her own mask and peer through the eyeholes. The voice that emerges is given shape and substance by the contours of the mask, which fits well or doesn't, although in time a mask may come to fit, as the face grows into its contours, becomes identified with the speaker."[9]

By becoming a priest, Hopkins put on a mask; by so doing he set aside his real self by surrendering himself not only to God but to Ignatius of Loyola, who would transform (the religious word is *formation*) Hopkins into a "soldier of Christ." As for Hopkins' poetic mask: he never felt at ease with it. He felt it was banal when juxtaposed to his priesthood. The conflict was likely the cause of much of his depression.

Indeed, although he often experienced great joy for beholding the beauty of the world, it was not enough to overcome his negative states of mind. There are some Hopkins scholars who have suggested that Hopkins might have been bipolar. I find this to be a distinct possibility.

Hopkins was not alone in being an artist of genius who was not recognized during his lifetime. Emily Dickinson, too, failed to have her poetry published and lived her life in obscurity. And Van Gogh sold only one or two of his paintings during his lifetime. If he had had just a little affirmation from others (and not just from his brother Theo), he may not have fallen into deeper and deeper depression, ending his life by suicide, a fate to which Hopkins nearly succumbed.

My reading of Adam Kirsch's "Back to Basics: How Gerard Manley Hopkins Remade English Poetry" (a review of Paul Mariani's biography) reveals a piercing insight about Hopkins' life: "Hopkins' life can be seen, in other words, as a slow-motion shipwreck, in which he was lost as surely as the nuns off the Kentish coast. But Mariani, a poet and a prolific biographer of poets, prefers not to see it that way."[10]

I am inclined to believe Kirsch has it right, but I will pass on further comment until I address the Terrible Sonnets. But I'll say now that, although I believe Hopkins' life on the whole was a tragic one, he has much to teach us about living, about being Christian, and about facing suffering. God graced him with moments of exquisite happiness and joy, but, to be frank, these moments were few and far between.

Mariani says that Hopkins the poet is just Hopkins the priest in another guise. This corresponds to Yeats's idea of the mask. The poet and the priest: two different masks. Which one was truer to the True Self of Gerard Manley Hopkins? This is the question that has caused debate among Hopkins critics. Many believe if he had not become a priest, Hopkins may have become a great poet while he lived, and he would have produced a larger body of work. But to argue this is futile. The fact is that Hopkins became a Jesuit and renounced poetry for a long time. We do have the right, however, to ask to what degree he damaged himself by suppressing his God-given talent.

I can't help seeing similarities between Hopkins and the Welsh poet R. S. Thomas. Thomas was Welsh; Hopkins joked about considering himself half-Welsh, so strongly did he identify with everything Welsh as a result of his time at St. Beuno's. Both tried to master the Welsh language. Both were poets entranced by birds. Hopkins' poems are filled with birds; the dominant one is the dove, which, of course, is the symbol of the Holy Spirit. Hopkins was capable of a kind of seeing similar to Zen "direct seeing." The difference between Hopkins and a Zen monk is that Hopkins' seeing was a sacramental one: to him everything was infused with and sparked by the Holy Spirit.

R. S. Thomas's poems are also filled with birds: he was an avid bird-watcher. He traveled to most of the bird sanctuaries of Great Britain and also to those outside the UK. Often his passion for bird-watching interfered with his role as a husband and a father, for so much time was devoted to his hobby that he neglected his wife and son.

Of course, birds and English poets are inextricably linked. Is it possible to think of Keats without the image of the nightingale coming to mind, or of Shelley without the skylark, or of Hardy without the "darkling thrush," or of the Anglo-Irish Yeats without the "wild swans at Coole"?

Birds are the symbol par excellence of the poetic experience, the bird that hovers between reality and imagination, heaven and earth, body and soul, hopes and dreams, life and death, and man and God.

George Santayana deeply understood the English love of birds. He writes:

> Their [birds'] life in the air is a sort of intoxication of innocence and happiness in the blind pulses of existence. They are voices of the morning, young hearts seeking experience and not remembering it; when they seem to sob they are only catching their breath. They spring from the ground as impetuously as a rocket or the jet of a fountain that bursts into a shower of sparks or of dew-drops; they circle as they rise soaring through veil after veil of luminous air, or dropping from level to level....Their rapture seems to us seraphic, not merely because it descends to us invisibly from a luminous height, straining our eyes and necks—in itself a cheap sublimity—but rather because birds sing so absolutely for the mad sake of singing.[11]

It's a shame that Santayana is not read much these days. He is an exquisite prose stylist, and some of his poetry is quite good. I became interested in him when I learned that he was a graduate of the school where I taught. I was also intrigued that he had often attended my parish church when he was a young man. He was attracted to our church because he was learning German, and the Jesuit priests preached in German. He was also appreciative of the church's music: the music was always excellent; many of the Germans were quite gifted musicians, some of them the founders of the famous and highly respected Boston Symphony.

Although R. S. Thomas and Hopkins shared a love of birds, they did not share religious doubt. Thomas was prone to religious doubt and struggled with it for most of his adult life. Like Tennyson's, his was a beleaguered faith. In this regard, Hopkins was more fortunate: his faith was securely anchored.

My novel *The Secret Dublin Diary of Gerard Manley Hopkins* is selling well in Ireland. I worked many years on it, and as a Catholic I often felt that by writing it I had perhaps stepped beyond appropriate boundaries. I sent a preliminary draft to a Jesuit, the Hopkins archivist at Oxford. A kind-hearted man, he sent me such an encouraging and approving letter. I had asked him if he would point out any biographical errors I may have made in my novel. He found one in a date, in which I was a year off. But more important, he enjoyed the narrative. It was his affirmation that inspired me to persevere as it took many years for me to find a publisher. Catholic publishing houses wouldn't touch my novel because it dealt with a controversial subject. I finally had to turn to a secular press, and I found the perfect one in Ireland, an interesting synchronicity, for Hopkins lived his last years as a university professor in Dublin.

I remember being disappointed when Ron Hansen's novel *Exiles* about Hopkins was published, for I wanted to be the first to have written a novel about the poet-priest. I also remember how excited I was to purchase Hansen's book, an author I greatly admired. Who can forget his magnificent *Mariette in Ecstasy*, an exquisitely beautiful novel, now a Catholic classic?

Exiles, however, disappointed me. Not because it's poorly written, for Hansen is incapable of an infelicitous sentence. I was let down because Hansen's narrative is more about the lives of the nuns who died on the steamship *Deutschland* than about Hopkins. He offers too much biographical information about the five Franciscan nuns, exiled (thus the title) by Bismarck's laws against Catholic religious orders; they were on their way to the United States to forge a new life in Missouri. Oh, I wish Hansen had written more about Hopkins, his life at Oxford, his conversion, his inner struggles, and his despair in Ireland. Well, he didn't, but I did. Let's hope that people will continue to purchase the book. Brisk sales when a book comes out do not mean it has staying power. About that only time will tell.

Now that Ted Kennedy has been buried, controversy has reared its ugly head here in Boston where Cardinal O'Malley is now being criticized for his role in the late senator's funeral. Conservative Catholics argue that Kennedy, who supported abortion rights, should not have been allowed a Catholic funeral Mass. Kennedy also supported gay rights, an issue brought to Cardinal O'Malley's attention by many Catholics from outside Massachusetts.

The cardinal's response was wise: "As archbishop of Boston, I considered it appropriate to represent the church at this liturgy out of respect for the senator, his family, those who attended the Mass and all those who were praying for the senator and his family at this difficult time. We are people of faith and we believe in a loving and forgiving God from whom we seek mercy" (*Boston Globe*).

Well, I am sure Ted is now resting in peace. But there are obviously many Catholics who are not at peace. But Kennedy loved much: he was a wonderful, loving father to his own children, and a father to his two brothers' children, and politically he fought for the poor. Who today fights for the poor? And because he loved much, he will, as Christ promised, be forgiven much.

I'm rereading "The Windhover."

The poem begins with "I." The ego is very present in the first moments of intense seeing. Hopkins has yet to lose himself in the beheld object. In fact, what truly occurs is the opposite of what he proclaims: "I caught." At the beginning, he thinks *he* has "caught" sight of the falcon flying in the sky. But the reality is that beauty has "caught him." This is not my insight but the French mystic Simone Weil's: she believed that God uses beauty to attract us to him. It's not a new insight; it goes back to St. Augustine, who likely borrowed it from someone else: God is the source of all beauty.

Speaking of ideas, I just received a lovely e-mail this morning from one of my best friends. He lives in Lyme Regis, England, one of the most beautiful locations I have ever beheld. He sent me a passage from one of Rev. Harry Emerson Fosdick's sermons:

Even some of us who do not think much of ourselves may have this high distinction that the supreme ideas of our time use us....The ultimate meaning of our lives...lies in the ideas which we allow to use us....We commonly think that a man gets his ideas, that they are his private property, his interior possession. No, ideas get us. They are historic, not we....In the end, there is no victory without being used by an idea whose time has come....What we do need is fresh vision of the overcoming powers in those ideas if we will have it so. In every generation the future has belonged to ideas in the air. They crucified Jesus, but one thing they could not do—injure his idea....My chief concern is not for the ultimate victory of good. My chief concern is lest in my generation I should somehow miss being used by the great ideas.[12]

Simone Weil's idea that beauty is a "snare: to bring us to God" is, again, not a new idea, but it used *her* to promulgate it. She also says in her essay "Forms of the Implicit Love of God" that beauty is Christ's "tender smile for us coming through matter," one that beckons us to him. These ideas are not only "useful" but beautiful of themselves.

As I reread "The Windhover," I am intrigued by Hopkins' initial reactions to the bird. First, it was the beauty of the bird that "caught" him, but an aesthetic joy turns to a more pragmatic appreciation when he states, "The mastery of the thing." By this he means the control by which the bird masters his flight in the air, how each movement is one of triumph over the elements—which are the wind, the air currents, and the earth's gravitation.

As a Jesuit, Hopkins had mastered nothing yet. Little did he know that he would fail his upcoming theology exam or that he would later be assigned to poor parishes, where he was overwhelmed by the degradations of the poverty and the vice of his parishioners. He was never a riveting preacher; his sermons were often too learned and above the comprehension of his flock. Even as a teacher at University College in Dublin, he was a failure, often the butt of his students' jokes. He was, as many of his Jesuit contemporaries repeated, an eccentric. He never really found his niche. Thus, mastery was something he admired and aspired to; but he himself was never a master of anything except poetry, where he was indeed a rare master, in fact, one of genius. But one must ask, Did he ever have an inkling of his genius? If he had ever received positive feedback about his poetry from more than one person (usually Canon Dixon, and not his best friend, Robert Bridges), he perhaps may have gained some confidence in his poetic power, but I believe he lived in a world of doubt regarding his poetic opus in which he always questioned its value and its purpose.

But if he truly thought his verse was useless, wouldn't he have ceased from writing it? This never happened, for he wrote to the very end of his life. His last poem was about Robert Bridges, whose opinion he so valued but who remained year after year so rarely affirming about his verse.

Hopkins' use of the word *mastery* also reminds me of the subtitle of the poem: "To Christ our Lord." Jesus is often referred to as the *Master*. The word today has assumed a pejorative meaning because of our country's history of slavery. Masters and slaves—just the idea angers many people. But for Jesus to be the Master simply means that he is the one to follow, the rabbi (teacher) to emulate. Hopkins' implicit wish in this poem is to be a man who has mastered being a Christian, a true follower of Christ.

Implicit in the poem is Hopkins' idea of *inscape*: the windhover does what it does best: being itself. With people, the same dynamic applies: we are at our best when we allow ourselves to *be* who we are. We are *not* ourselves when we *pretend* to be other than who we are, which applies not only to our personality but to our human gifts and talents as well. The more we achieve "mastery" of our innate gifts, the more we glorify Jesus Christ, our Lord and Savior, which ironically is not really a case of mastering as it is one of "letting it be."

As an example—and I say this humbly—I knew that I had a flair for teaching. And I made it my business to permit myself to become the best teacher I could be. If I believed my evaluations and the feedback that I'd received from others, I allowed myself to *be* myself. To do otherwise wouldn't have been *true* to myself; therefore, I had an obligation to allow my talent to bloom, to nurture it in the ways needed. Thus, to say one has *mastered* something is not a vain boast: to master cooking, to master a sport, to master a language, to master music or art is a legitimate thing to be proud of, because to master anything is to allow an innate talent to blossom. Which doesn't mean we have to go around boasting about our ability, but we shouldn't be ashamed of it either. Humility is truth.

Hopkins was ordained in September 1877. Afterward he had a number of assignments: Mount St. Mary's (1877—78), back to Stonyhurst, then on to the Immaculate Conception and Farm Street (1878), both in the prestigious section of Mayfair, London. He also served briefly in a parish church in Oxford (1879); then he went to Bedford Leigh and slum parishes in Liverpool and Glasgow (1880—81).

The Jesuits quite simply didn't know what to do with Hopkins. One assumes that they must've known that he was intellectually brilliant. To win a first in classics at Balliol, Oxford, is no mean feat. They failed to find a way, however, to put his brilliance to use; they should have steered him into an academic life, which would have allowed him to blossom as a teacher. And it would have been a wonderful opportunity for Jesuit seminarians to be taught by one of the great intellectuals of the Victorian period.

In the end, the Society of Jesus sent him to University College in Dublin, not so much to teach, but to correct exams in the classics:

drudge work that nearly killed Hopkins. For a man such as Hopkins, being sent to Ireland must have been like banishment; an ardent patriot, he greatly loved his country, and by being sent to Dublin, he left behind his family, his friends, and his beloved country. If his years at St. Beuno's College were his *Paradiso*, his years in Dublin were his *Inferno*.

America magazine is advertising its annual Foley Poetry Contest. I've entered my own poem about Hopkins. The first prize is $1,000, and the three runners-up will have their poems published in *America*. I believe my poem is a good one. I'll have to wait to see if it is worthy of publication.

Offspring

Dearest Gerard,
You are not a eunuch.
        Never!
Your offspring
Have spread worldwide.
You'd be delighted
To know that you too
Shine like shook foil
Dazzling many an eye
With the beauty of you,
Who never chose
Not to be, but to praise
To your last breath.

The Dublin Years

I have come to Hopkins' assignment to Dublin. I know from my previous reading that these years in Ireland will be the unhappiest years of his life, and Dublin will be the place of his far-too-early death. It will be difficult for me to plunge again into the Terrible Sonnets, but I long abided with the Hopkins of these poems when I wrote my novella about him. Perhaps I shall win new insights about his life and the cause or causes of his depression.

I just had a telephone interview with a radio program host in Ireland. She asked me whether I believed that Hopkins had somehow resolved what had troubled him in the Terrible Sonnets. There is no definitive answer. But the Jesuits are on record with their description of his deathbed scene. When he was dying, he is reported to have said, "I am so happy. I am so happy."

Today is December 7, the anniversary of the wreck of the *Deutschland*.

In 1882, Father William Delany, SJ, the then president-elect of the new University College, Dublin, needed Jesuit scholars to staff what he hoped would one day be a match for Trinity College, which was then closed to Catholics. Delany had been warned by the Irish provincial Father Tuite not to staff his new college with professors from England, especially during this time of debate over Home Rule in Ireland. But Delany was intent on success and wrote to the English province, pleading for qualified professors. Delany received a reply recommending

Hopkins, who "is very clever and a good scholar....[but] I should be doing you no kindness in sending you a man so eccentric. I am trying him this year in coaching B.A.s at Stonyhurst, but with fear and trembling."[1] Hopkins knew nothing of this. He also knew nothing of the letter sent to Delany by Father George Porter, English assistant to the Jesuit General in Rome. Porter wrote: "I think Fr. Purbrick might be induced to let you have Hopkins or [J. T.] Walford: I do not think he would part with [Joseph] Rickaby or [Herbert] Lucas. Hopkins is clever, well-trained, teaches well but has never succeeded well: his mind runs in eccentric ways."[2]

So let's review this scenario: Names are mentioned for the post in Ireland. Some are the cream of the crop, but only two will really be considered as appointees: Walford and Hopkins. Hopkins knew Walford, who had been a junior master at Eton, taught at Newman's Oratory School, and, like Hopkins, was a convert. Notice that in both letters Hopkins is the recipient of faint praise: he is clever but eccentric. Then there is the paradox of describing him as one who "teaches well" but has never "succeeded well." No one mentions that Hopkins had been dubbed the "star of Balliol" at Oxford. No one mentions that he had won a first in Greats. He is merely "clever" but to offset that even further, he is offhandedly described and diminished as "eccentric"—without further explanation. So the man they sent to Dublin was the man they didn't want or need in England. Hopkins was dispensable.

Although Hopkins may have not known the backroom politics of the decision-making process that sent him to Ireland, he likely figured it out when he discovered the nature of his job: grading hundreds of exams.

The vow of obedience is one of three major vows—the others are poverty and chastity—taken by members of Catholic religious orders. To disobey his Jesuit superiors would never have entered Hopkins' mind, unlike Thomas Merton, who, though he was generally obedient, was occasionally allowed to bend the rules because of his renown. Hopkins, however, never achieved fame in his lifetime, and he was not from an eminent family; thus, no exceptions were made for him, and he meekly did what he was told—down to the smallest matters.

Although assigned to the college's classics chair, Hopkins spent most of his time not on his lectures but on grading the endless exams that crossed his desk. His eyes were so impaired from reading so many thousands of exams that he feared he was going blind. He was eventually forced to wear glasses. To be fair in evaluating his Irish students (who were not fair to him, being rude and rowdy), he had devised a scrupulous grading system that aimed for the perfect score, a system that nearly drove him mad. He was often seen wearing a wet-towel turban on his head to treat the headaches from which he constantly suffered.

In my opinion, it was unwise to appoint him to such a position because Hopkins was physically fragile, and this was well known in the Jesuit community. His superiors certainly knew he was "eccentric," but they also knew he was not physically strong. Furthermore, they knew he was the archetypal English gentleman/intellectual, for Hopkins was very much interested in what constituted a gentleman, as shown in his letters to his friend Bridges. His preoccupation with the concept may, of course, be the result of his reading Newman's essay "The Gentleman," with its famous opening line, "It is almost a definition of a gentleman to say he is one who never inflicts pain."

Hopkins was indeed a gentleman (a gentle man), and if Campion Hall, the Jesuit college of Oxford University founded in 1896, had existed during his lifetime, he should have taught at Oxford, where his intellectual brilliance would have been appreciated and his eccentricities relished. Again, if he had not chosen Scotus over Aquinas in his theological exam, his life as a Jesuit would have been far easier and likely more productive.

I've returned to my library copy of Hopkins' letters to Bridges. Although he likely knew nothing of the politics of his appointment that reached as far as Rome, once he landed in Dublin Hopkins must have learned how controversial his appointment truly was. He wrote to Bridges that there had been "a bitter row" over his election.[3] It seems that it had been narrowed down to two candidates for the classics chair: a Father Reffe and Father Hopkins. This must not have pleased Hopkins, who surely was disturbed to discover that there was an important faction of the Jesuit order that didn't want him in Ireland.

It's no wonder that his first letters in 1884 to his friend Bridges were so gloomy, so filled with a depression that lasted the whole time he remained as a teacher at University College. He described himself as being "in great weakness"[4] and, at one point, as "recovering from a deep fit of nervous prostration" that had him thinking he was dying.[5] At one point he feared he was going mad and longed for the relief that only change, which he seldom got, could bring.[6]

Father Delany later commented that Hopkins suffered nervous depression for his entire stay there. He then compared Hopkins to another Jesuit, who suffered from epilepsy. Both men died, according to Delany, at an early age.

In a letter to Bridges, Hopkins wrote that he "must absolutely have encouragement as much as crops rain," but that the ordinary circumstances of his life were such that not even any amount of encouragement could inspire him to continue with his play *Winefred's Well* "or anything else." After a long silence, he said, he had written two sonnets; "If ever anything was written in blood one of these was."[7]

The footnote to this letter in the printed collection indicates that Robert Bridges believed that the sonnet written "in blood" was "Carrion Comfort." But no one can with certainty know which two sonnets Hopkins was referring to.[8]

I'm reading Hopkins' "Epithalamion," which he began composing to celebrate his brother Everard's marriage, but never finished. It should be noted that Hopkins had a tremendous respect for marriage. He was overjoyed when he learned in Dublin that his dearest friend Robert Bridges was soon to marry. Hopkins felt it was the state to which a man was called. But I think there was more to it than that: he understood loneliness, and he feared it for his friend. So when he read the letter announcing the imminent marriage, Hopkins wrote to Bridges, "I have a kind of spooniness and delight over married people." He enjoyed hearing people say "my wife," and "my husband," or "shew me the wedding ring."[9]

I am sure he was somewhat envious that most people have such intimacy with someone. Marriage is the norm for most people. But I suspect that, in his heart of hearts, it meant something very special for Hopkins to be able to say of his Oxford peer, "my friend Bridges." Hopkins highly valued his friendships. It's one of the reasons Dublin was so difficult for him. He never truly became part of the circle of friends who taught at University College, primarily because they viewed him as odd and ineffectual.

The biographer Robert Bernard Martin comments on Hopkins' tenure at University College this way:

It is hard to ignore the barely concealed hostility to Hopkins in the denials of his brother Jesuits of his being overworked, even if it is no longer certain what had caused their resentment. The

Jesuit history of the College shifts all the blame to Hopkins' shoulders saying that he perhaps "ought never to have been a Jesuit," and that "though he had many trials to endure, they were mainly due to his highly-wrought temperament."[10]

Today the Jesuits are very proud to include Hopkins among their most prestigious members, a far cry from their earlier estimations of the "eccentric" whom nobody really wanted, either as a professor or as a parish priest.

Few readers of poetry during Hopkins' life would've seen or appreciated his genius. He was writing a new kind of verse, and the world wasn't quite ready for it. Critics today are reestimating Hopkins by claiming that he was truly a Victorian poet. But to me, Hopkins is a modern poet. He didn't speak to the Victorians (not successfully, anyway), but he speaks to us, readers of the twentieth and twenty-first centuries. About that I have no doubt.

Hopkins considered his poem "Epithalamion" to be an allegory. He used the water to represent the bride and the naked swimming boys as the groom. It is an odd analogy, but not so strange when one takes into consideration that Hopkins admitted to a class of Irish students that he had never seen a naked woman. But later, in a letter to his brother Arthur, the artist, he quite clinically critiques his brother's portrait of a female, finding fault with both the "breast and nipples." Hopkins may have never seen a naked woman, but he definitely knew her form and shape!

In his poem "Song of Myself," Hopkins' contemporary Walt Whitman presents a woman who from her curtained window secretly watches naked men and boys swim. Hopkins (the stranger in the poem "Epithalamion") also watches the boys swimming from a distance. Section 11 of Whitman's poem describes the scene thus:

Twenty-eight young men bathe by the shore,
Twenty-eight young men all so friendly,
Twenty-eight years of womanly life and all so lonesome.
The young men float on their backs, their white bellies
        bulge to the
Sun, they do not ask who seizes fast to them,
They do not know who puffs and declines with pendant and
        bending arch
They do not think whom they souse with spray.[11]

Whitman makes it quite clear that the woman who is peeking at
the naked males does so not from lust but from being "so lonesome"—something to consider while reading Hopkins' similarly
located poem about boys swimming naked. He had never been as
lonely in his life as he was during his time in Dublin. Surely the
many happy memories of skinny-dipping with his youthful friends,
his Oxford friends, and his Jesuit friends must've all coalesced when
he commenced writing his brother's wedding poem, "Epithalamion."

Here are a few lines from "Epithalamion," so similar to Whitman's
but portrayed in very different language:

By there comes a listless stranger: beckoned by the noise
He drops towards the river: unseen
Sees the bevy of them, how the boys
With dare and with downdolphinry and bellbright bodies
        huddling out,
Are earthworld, airworld, waterworld thorough hurled, all by
        turn and turn about.

The noise is the shouts of the ebullient boys at play. Hopkins is likely remembering his own many swims with friends and seminarians in the tree-lined, rock-strewn Hodder River at Stonyhurst. These were surely some of his happiest moments in life as he and the other males delighted in the joy and freedom of swimming, diving, dunking, and "huddling out." I love his made-up alliterative word-metaphor *downdolphinry* to describe the diving exploits. There is a journal note about his staring too long at a friend during such a skinny-dip. This friend must have been someone whose physical beauty Hopkins was especially attracted to—thus a "sin" against his practice of "custody of the eyes." Hopkins scrupulously recorded his sins, part of the examination of conscience every Jesuit daily made. No deed or thought escaped Hopkins' inner eye. One wished he could have practiced a reverse "custody of eyes" that would have allowed him to live without the constant burden of believing he might be sinning. How enervating it must have been for him; thus, one's heart cannot fail to feel compassion for this beautiful, gifted, holy soul, overburdened by a preoccupation with sin.

What a blessing it would have been if Hopkins had had the good fortune to discover, as had Merton, the compassionate mystic Lady Julian of Norwich. Her holy message would have been cool rain to Hopkins' parched soul. Merton himself had followed the Ignatian exercises at his Perry Street apartment before his entry into Gethsemani, until he discovered John of the Cross. But he later embraced the message of Lady Julian, who became his favorite mystic.

I believe Merton turned to Lady Julian because, as a Trappist, he already had plenty of asceticism in his life (Trappists are famous for it); what he needed was a mystic who stressed not so much sin but love, especially unconditional love. Merton, burdened too long by the onus of guilt, finally found some relief from his burden in Lady

Julian's *Revelations of Divine Love*. He writes, "The theology of Lady Julian is a theology of the all-embracing totality and fullness of divine love. This is, for her, the ultimate Reality, in the light of which all created being and all the vicissitudes of life and of history fade into unimportance."[12]

Lady Julian is my favorite mystic as well because her message to us Christians is so optimistic. I learned about her through T. S. Eliot's *Four Quartets*. In his last quartet, "Little Gidding," he quotes her verbatim: "All manner of thing shall be well and / All manner of thing shall be well."[13] I am forever grateful for Eliot's introduction to one of the greatest mystics of Christianity. However, I do recall now a priest discouraging me from reading her, for he thought she was an Anglican! This was not unusual, for before Lady Julian became famous in the latter part of the twentieth century, few Catholics knew anything about her. I recall the Christian apologist Baron Friedrich von Hügel chastising his niece in a letter for thinking that Lady Julian of Norwich was an Anglican:

> As to Mother Julian, where on earth has my Gwen-child acquired the notion that she was an Anglican! An Anglican in A.D. 1360? My Gwen, we must do some Church history later on! Of course she accepted the Pope as she accepted Christ and as she accepted God.[14]

Being a bit prone to depression myself, I enter the "wintry world" of Hopkins' Terrible Sonnets with a bit of trepidation, but I've survived other encounters with these poems, and I will survive this one too. Let's first address why his sonnets are called "terrible." The term for them was first used by Hopkins' best friend, Robert Bridges. Critic W. H. Gardner preferred to describe them as "the Sonnets of

Desolation," and the critic N. H. MacKenzie has called them "the Dark Sonnets."

Bridges' term "Terrible Sonnets" has been the one to have endured, as it should, for he was the man responsible for saving Hopkins' poetry and finally having it published.

Well, today I had a nice surprise. I was resting when I heard the doorbell ring. At first, I was annoyed because I was tired and was in no mood for visitors. But it was FedEx with a large package for which I had to sign. I wasn't sure what it could be until I remembered that Father Bill McNichols said my icon would likely be ready in April.

I eagerly opened the package and had to use scissors to cut the layers of bubble wrap and then the final covering of wax paper: there emerged the most beautiful image of Gerard Manley Hopkins I'd ever seen. McNichols not only captured his face but was able to suggest the holiness of the priest-poet. I couldn't have been happier, and I must now write him a letter thanking him for the icon, one I commissioned myself to commemorate my novella based on the life of Hopkins while he lived and taught in Dublin, Ireland. Father Bill has entitled the icon *Hopkins among the Fire-Folk.* The phrase is from Hopkins' poem "The Starlight Night," which lately has become one of my favorite Hopkins poems.

Father Bill framed it beautifully and prepared it to be hung on a wall, but I have a beautiful mahogany easel, the perfect place for it in my living room. Thus, I can share it with my relatives and friends who will surely be impressed by its beauty. Father Bill outdid himself in "writing" this icon!

Father Bill is without doubt one of the world's greatest iconographers, an artist who has been universally praised not only for the beauty of his work but also for his courage: he has been under fire from some people for writing icons of Princess Diana and Matthew Sheppard. I've seen these two icons and still don't know what all the fuss is about: they are beautiful, and in their unique ways both people deserve to called blessed people, for they both possessed saintly personalities. There are many saintly (iconic) people in the world who haven't been canonized, and Father Bill recognizes this fact, and I personally am glad he does.

Another interesting fact about the Terrible Sonnets: critics cannot determine with certitude the chronology of their composition. Hopkins seemingly had no sonnet sequence in mind when he began to compose them, so it's guesswork on our part to figure out when they were written because Hopkins did not date them. But in the end it doesn't make much difference: they are poems that shed light on his time in Dublin, a limited time of four years. It's possible that most of them were written in 1885, a particularly unhappy time for Hopkins. But again, we can only surmise the dates.

I lived with these sonnets for a long time when I wrote my novella about Hopkins. These poems are heartrending in the nakedness of their pain. I can't think of any other poet so candid about his spiritual and psychological state, unless one jumps to the twentieth century's confessional poets like Sylvia Plath, Anne Sexton, and John Berryman.

In Victorian times, however, poets just didn't bare their souls. Yes, they would write about love and suffering and death in a general way. For instance, Tennyson's "In Memoriam" is a moving elegy for his friend Arthur Hallam, but details about their friendship are scarce. Tennyson indeed allows us a glimpse (a rather long one!) of his pain, but only that.

With Hopkins' sonnets, we have his pain in more detail than Tennyson's. Hopkins needed to open himself to his best friend because it was the only way he could survive. If he did not reveal his pain, it is possible that his depression would have deepened.

I take Hopkins at his poems' words, and they are quite plain in their significance. I will not play games with their meaning. As I said at the beginning of this journal, Hopkins was not trapped in a mystical dark night of the soul. Something far more sinister was going on within his soul and mind. And everyone must be willing (and honest) to face the darkness of these sonnets and try to unearth the reasons for it.

I've come across people who love Hopkins and his verse and who react with outrage at the suggestion that he may have been tempted to kill himself. They want to believe that, as a priest, he would never consider such a despairing deed. I try to explain that while he was a priest, he was also human and terribly lonely. In addition, he had referred to himself as "time's eunuch" and longed to "beget" art, but felt he had accomplished nothing of note in his life, either as a priest or as an artist.

I believe that the first of the Terrible Sonnets is the one that begins, "To seem the stranger lies my lot, my life / Among strangers." Many critics, of course, interpret this opening line to refer to Hopkins' banishment to Dublin from his beloved England. No one should underestimate Hopkins' love for his country. He thoroughly identified with being an Englishman. He not only loved his country, its history, and its literature, but he also loved its physical attributes, the rolling English countryside and its spectacular skyscape. The only thing he didn't love about England was its falling away from the Roman Catholic Church.

Hopkins is fully aware of the biblical significance of his first line: Moses described himself as a "stranger in a strange land" when he lived in Midian (Book of Exodus). It simply means that he was not among his own people. Neither was Hopkins: he now lived with the Irish, who at the time were held in contempt by most Englishmen because they still clung to their Catholic faith; they had not bent to Henry VIII or to Cromwell, and they had not bent since.

Hopkins' description of himself, however, went beyond politics, nationalism, and religion. His lot in life had often been that of a stranger. He was now in his forties, living in Dublin. It is not unreasonable to think that he was looking back on his life and, perhaps for the first time, when many adults experience midlife crises, realized how often he had been an outsider.

Hopkins' life as a Jesuit was certainly "strange": He was not a cradle Catholic, as most of his brother Jesuits were. He was a convert. Cradle Catholics often have a superior attitude toward converts: they are tolerant, but at the same time often feel that the status of a convert is not quite equal to that of a born Catholic. And now that Hopkins was in Ireland, *the* Catholic country, he would indeed again have felt like a stranger. He seemingly didn't belong to any group except, of course, the two he was naturally born into: his family and England.

He lamented being removed from his mother, father, brothers, and sisters. We must remember that he was the eldest of eight children, a large family. By all accounts it was a lively family, ebullient with play, laughter, and love. This was the family he gave up when he chose to become a Catholic: his family was most vehemently opposed to his conversion. And when he converted to Catholicism, he came close to not winning his degree from Oxford, a university that did not allow Catholics, and thus he lost forever his chance for a brilliant academic career that surely would have been his. And now, added to this, was his physical removal from the family and the country that nurtured him.

We can only wonder if Hopkins had a inkling about what his conversion would do to him, and to both his inner and outer life—and to his family. Had he truly realized the extent to which he would become a stranger by his decision? I tend to think he might have underestimated the ramifications of his decision. One person who truly understood what he was about to give up by his conversion was John Henry Newman, which explains Newman's advice to both Hopkins and Dolben not to approach their conversion in a hasty manner. Yes, Newman was a great Catholic apologist, as shown by his masterful autobiography, but in dealing with people on a one-on-one basis he was not the type of priest who quickly pushed people into the Church. He always advised candidates to ponder slowly their decision to convert, always emphasizing that there was no need to rush into things. Hopkins did not take Newman's advice. He became a Catholic rather quickly. As to Dolben, he died before he could convert, but I suspect he too was about to ignore Newman' advice and was eager to be accepted into the Church.

At the age of twenty-two, then, Hopkins converted to the Catholic faith, thereby choosing to enter what most of his countrymen considered the ultimate strange land: the Roman Catholic Church. Why?

Hopkins surely felt he was being faithful to what Merton refers to as the True Self. He fervently believed in the Real Presence; thus, he was convinced that the Catholic Church was the true Church. He also believed that not being a member of the Catholic Church imperiled his immortal soul. The latter alone would have caused him to rush into the arms of the Church. We cannot forget that most Catholics then (and many even today) literally believed that outside the Church there was no salvation.

At the end of the first stanza of "To seem a stranger," Hopkins mentions Christ. He had a lover in Christ, but often even Christ was not always his peace: here, Hopkins describes him as his "sword and strife." In the next stanza Hopkins lovingly speaks of his country, even stranger (estranged) to him now that he lived in Ireland. England was, to use his metaphor, the "wife" of his creativity. Indeed, most of his greatest poetry was written in England (he could not have known that his Terrible Sonnets would supersede his previous verse, poetry that contains, to borrow Yeats' phrase, "a terrible beauty"), but England would not "hear" him.

No amount of "pleading" on his part ever won him a hearing of his verse, although keep in mind that he was also ambivalent about publication: he fiercely desired it but when his friend Canon Dixon offered to have his poetry included in an anthology, Hopkins rejected his kind offer. But it still must have been heartbreaking to have his own order reject his poetry. And it surely reinforced another aspect of his strangeness: his poetry was also judged (like him) as eccentric, or rather not poetry at all, a rejection that surely wounded him grievously. One wonders why he even continued to write poetry. Yet, I believe that he had to write because it helped him survive. Of course, I don't rule out the contribution of his Jesuit spirituality in helping him endure his time in Dublin: he was a holy man, and God's grace surely was granted to him to overcome these dark days. God also granted him his writing talent, an outlet whose value we should not underestimate.

The third stanza of this poem begins with Hopkins stating an inescapable fact: "I am in Ireland now." He was making every effort to face the reality of his life: *I'm not living in my beloved England, but here in Ireland, and so I must accept it.* And even though he was not where he would rather have been, he could still love people: "Kind love both give and get." He appears to be saying: *I'm still human, I'm still a priest, I'm now a teacher; and as a priest and as a teacher, I can affirm and love even if I am not affirmed and loved. In short, I can emulate the One I most love: Jesus Christ.*

William Styron, in his autobiographical *Darkness Visible*, believes that much depression is the result of actual loss or imagined future losses: "Loss in all of its manifestations is the touchstone of depression—in the progress of the disease and, most likely, in its origin....At a later date I would gradually be persuaded that devastating loss in childhood figured as a probable genesis of my own disorder; meanwhile...I felt loss at every hand."[15]

However dark the Terrible Sonnets are, they can serve as a life-saver for those trapped in the same state of being, for the sonnets are not only about anguish and despair but also about triumph.

The second of the Terrible Sonnets—"I wake and feel the fell of dark, not day"—has preoccupied me for two days. It's a much darker, depressed poem than the first. Here Hopkins, who loved the exterior world so much, barely refers to the outside landscape. These are primarily poems of an inner landscape, and it's not pretty: it's not a land flowing with milk and honey. It's a precursor of T. S. Eliot's *The Waste Land*.

In the poem, when he awakes (did he really sleep or just think he did?), it's daytime, but he is still in the grip of inner darkness. He is depressed, and he feels the "fell of dark." I'm going with the traditional definition of "fell": darkness has fallen upon him. But out of curiosity, I went to the dictionary. The word also means: *verb*, to kill; *adjective*, of an inhumanly cruel nature, fierce, capable of destroying, lethal, sharp and biting; *noun*, the hide of an animal, a pelt.

This darkness that befell Hopkins wasn't a gentle fall of rain or snow. It was more like the attack of some fierce animal, and it was tearing him to pieces.

Haven't written an entry for several days. I received an emergency call from the nursing home where my mother has lived for the last two years. She was at the brink of death, but to my surprise, and that of the nurses and doctors, she has since rallied. She still has a strong will to live. Although it would be a mercy for her to go to God, she's seemingly not ready to leave this world.

She's had profound dementia for several years, and she knows no one in her family. I think she still knows me, but sometimes I'm not even certain about that. It's now a waiting game, and anything can happen. I still manage to visit her every day at the nursing home where she receives excellent care.

Today, for the first time in five days, I have the energy to address Hopkins' second Terrible Sonnet. After experiencing my own "fell of dark" (my mother's near-death experience), I'm now prepared to face Hopkins' darkness.

"And my lament / Is cries countless, cries like dead letters sent / To dearest him that lives alas! away." Who is this "dearest him"? It is generally acknowledged as a reference to Digby Dolben. Dolben never answered the endless letters that Hopkins had written; nevertheless, Dolben remained "dearest him." I believe that here Hopkins laments not having connected with his friend: his cries of the heart went unheard and unanswered, and this lack of response from someone he dearly loved has dragged him into deeper darkness, for the light of his life then had been Dolben, and the light was no longer present.

One might also assume that the "him" is Christ, in which case Hopkins felt abandoned by his spiritual lover. As with an unresponsive human lover, Christ isn't (it seemed to Hopkins) responding to his "cries countless": his prayers, his vows of love, his pleas for answers to his prayers, his cries for spiritual consolation; the only response, silence.

The third of the Terrible Sonnets begins: "No worst, there is none. Pitched past pitch of grief, / More pangs will, schooled at forepangs, wilder wring." Before I go further, I should mention that I've been rereading Paul Mariani's masterful *Commentary on the Poems of Hopkins.* Although Bridges thought that "Carrion Comfort" was the sonnet "written in blood," Mariani opines that it was actually "No worst, there is none." Mariani writes: "For in this sonnet alone there is no hope, no underlying comfort for the speaker in knowing that he is suffering with a purpose, as he realizes in 'Carrion Comfort.' The poem is all darkness."[16]

There's such power and agony in the opening declarative sentence: "No worst, there is none." Edgar, in Shakespeare's *King Lear*, says, "The worst is not / So long as we can say 'This is the worst'" (4.1.27 — 28). But Hopkins is declaring that we can *never* say, "This is the worst"—in other words, things can always get even worse than they are now.

Hopkins was a dilettante when it came to music (he composed many songs) and because of his psychological state of mind, by "pitch of grief" he was likely referring to the lowest note made by a musical instrument. Pitch is also a sports term, bringing to mind a tossed ball. One also thinks of a ship pitching in a storm (as in *The Wreck of the Deutschland*) and of the deep black color of pitch or tar. The question here: To what place has Hopkins been pitched if it's *beyond* grief? What's beyond grief? He doesn't know yet because his grief and pain are still being "schooled," exquisitely honed to bring to him even more grief and agony. And there's nothing he can do about it.

Well, not exactly. He does what he's always done when sorely troubled: he prays to Christ, but this time no comforting arrives after his praying. He begs, "Comforter, where, where is your comforting?"

It's such a heartrending question, especially the repetition of *where*. One cannot help remembering Christ's promise to abide with us always, and his invitation to all who are weary—to come to him, and he will give us rest. Even Hopkins' prayers to the Blessed Mother prove hopeless: "Mary, mother of us, where is your relief?"

In the next line he returns to the word *cries*, one that dominated the former sonnet; but now it is his "cries countless" that seem never to end: they "heave, herds-long," a line that suggests a seemingly endless train of bison or caribou wending its way through the landscape.

"I feel the fell of dark": Here, Hopkins is so enveloped by darkness, by "pitch," that he can feel its cold, menacing touch. Darkness renders him blind, his hands reaching out, imploring gestures to both Christ and Mary to come quickly to his rescue, as the Franciscan nun on the *Deutschland* cried, "O Christ, Christ, come quickly." It seems that "wórld-sorrow" has overcome Hopkins, pounding him upon a worldly surface, as a blacksmith would pound upon "an age-old anvil" making it "wince and sing."

In the sestet, Hopkins confesses that the "mind has mountains; cliffs of fall / Frightful, sheer, no-man-fathomed." I instantly thought of King Lear when I read these verses, and returned to my volume to find the exact allusion. It appears when Gloucester intends to kill himself by tossing himself from the Cliffs of Dover to instant death. His son Edgar, disguised as a beggar, describes the cliff's fall to his father. (Gloucester is really not at the edge of the cliffs, but being blind, thinks he is; his son is attempting to "trick" his father out of his despondency and despair.) Edgar speaks: "Here's the place. Stand still. How fearful / And dizzy 'tis to cast one's eyes so low! / The crows and choughs that wing the midway air / Show scarce so gross as beetles" (4.6.11—14).

Poor, blind Gloucester, for whom the world has become too cruel, too dark, and too fearful a place to abide in, carefully listens, but the frightening description does not dampen his resolution to end his life.

For poor Hopkins, too, the world had also become too dark, the "mind cliffs" he clung to were "no-man-fathomed": no man had ever known such a dreadful place, one that had never been measured, and there was no place for him to flee for shelter, for protection. Like Gloucester, Hopkins was homeless with no place to rest his head. Like Gloucester, he was a "wretch" who crept his "dusty way to death." Hopkins concludes the poem thus: "Life death does end and each day dies with sleep." His only consolation is that life ends and each day ends in sleep. The darkness of unconsciousness (sleep) is preferable to being awake, but death itself would be better, for then it is an absolute ending.

This is, to me, the most despairing of the Terrible Sonnets. Even his next sonnet, "Carrion Comfort," isn't as bleak because, there, a crack of light appears, miniscule but present. Even though I've already addressed this poem, let's briefly revisit it: "Not, I'll not, carrion comfort, Despair, not feast on thee."

Some critics interpret "Carrion Comfort" in a more triumphant fashion than I do. I see no triumph: Hopkins has not overcome his depression; he has simply come to a pause with his "wrestling." The battle is far from over. Thus the hopeful aspect of the poem is that Hopkins has somehow found enough strength within him not to cry, "I can no more." He has a smidgen of strength left in him "not to choose not to be."

Shakespeare's tragedy *Hamlet* and its famous soliloquy, "To be or not to be," immediately comes to mind. That Hopkins would identify with Hamlet in this sonnet (even employing his words) is not far-fetched, for Hamlet understood full well that to kill himself would cause him to suffer eternal damnation for his sin of despair. It's his fear of hell that ultimately stops Hamlet's hand from thrusting a "bare bodkin" into his heart.

Hopkins' next lines go on to question God: *Why have you so brutalized me,* he seems to ask, *abandoning me alone in a heap upon a field so frightened that I must do all I can to avoid you?* This is such a heartrending, almost heart-stopping question to come from a priest—a priest who is now imagining his adversary to be God himself, who treats his priest abominably for reasons he cannot in the least fathom.

We cannot help being moved by his poignant questions. Like him, we are completely confused as to why Hopkins has been nearly stomped to death by Despair's "wring-world right foot" and opposed by "a lionlimb against me." It's as if he has been mauled by some huge, voracious animal as he now lies alone in a heap with tempestuous winds blowing over him; it reminds me of King Lear in his madness upon the heath, howling against the elements, where he believes abide the gods.

In the sestet, a bewildered and weary Hopkins tries to understand *why* he is being so brutally punished and pummeled. *Why?* Because he has been an obedient follower: "I kissed the rod / Hand rather...." But like winnowed (beaten) chaff, he is blown away to who knows where. He concludes that he is merely a wretch who has wrestled "with (my God!) my God." In his feeling of having been utterly forsaken, he echoes our greatest human sufferer, Jesus Christ, who cried out from the cross, "My God, my God, why have you abandoned me?"

Of course, one can interpret "Carrion Comfort" as a triumphant poem: Hopkins was still alive, still writing poems. Despite what he was suffering, he absolutely refused to succumb to, to feast on, that "carrion comfort" that is despair.

The Latin epigraph (Jer 12:1) that opens the next sonnet—beginning "*Justus quidem tu es, Domine*"—is translated as follows: "Thou art always in the right, Eternal One, when I complain to thee; yet I would argue this with thee—Why do bad men prosper? Why are scoundrels secure and serene? Thou plantest them and they take root, they flourish, yes, and they bear fruit."

One of my Jesuit friends, who is also a theologian, doesn't admire this sonnet; he grudgingly describes it as a "beautiful whine." An intriguing oxymoron! Is Hopkins whining in this sonnet? To be candid, there is about it a "woe is me" element. It reminds me of the cliché of those struck unexpectedly with suffering who instantly cry out, "Why me?" A friend of mine who was struck down with incurable cancer corrected me when I asked why her. She answered, "Why not me?" I admired her for her pluck and acceptance of her fate, for she indeed died of her disease.

Hopkins speaks directly to his Lord, and reminds him that usually he (Hopkins) stands up for the Lord as being just, but in his own case he sees no justice. Hopkins calls the Lord "Sir" as a sign of Victorian respect, but it also establishes a distance between the two as if Hopkins doesn't quite trust his Lord, reminding him that although "sinners' ways prosper," he himself has met with "disappointment" in all his endeavors. Furthermore, who would address an intimate as "sir"? With friends like the Lord, Hopkins suggests, who needs enemies?

Here in Dublin Hopkins felt defeated, and that his Lord was out to "thwart" him. All his efforts to be a good Christian seemed wasted; nothing good thrived. Moreover, he hadn't been able to write any worthwhile poetry (little did he know that he would be remembered for the Terrible Sonnets). His most fruitful time in Wales was long gone.

In the next lines, Hopkins looks about him and notices that nature is always fertile, still produces: "See, banks and brakes / Now, leavèd how thick! Lacèd they are again / With fretty chervil, look, and fresh wind shakes /Them." He notices that birds still build their nests, but he builds *nothing* even though he strains to produce something; time has rendered him a "eunuch."

Finally, he utters to his Lord his most poignant cry of the heart and soul: "Send my roots rain."

Is this sonnet the whine of a neurotic? To a degree I must agree with my Jesuit friend. Hopkins had periods of inspiration and had written poetry of great beauty. It's true that the muse seemingly abandoned him in Dublin. But he was well taken care of by the Jesuits. Daily Hopkins saw the homeless walking Dublin's streets and loitering (and drinking) in their parks, where many of them set up living quarters under trees and within shrubbery. But he himself was clothed, sheltered, and fed well by his community.

Hopkins' greatest desire was to create "one work that wakes"; that is, a poem bursting with life. How could he when he himself was lifeless? He was projecting his frustration upon his Lord, charging him with being unjust. Hopkins, quite frankly, was here overcome with self-pity. He was an unhappy man, lacking the energy to compose any notable verse (the paradox is that he *was composing* the Terrible Sonnets, his lifesaver). Without his realizing it, his Lord had in fact sent his roots rain! But he was so self-involved in how much he suffered that he could not see that he was the recipient of his Lord's grace.

So yes, his sonnet is a "beautiful whine," and we cannot escape its pain. Hopkins felt that his life was a waste, that even plants and birds were more productive than he, a priest of the Church. He also felt like a failure as a poet because he was not writing the kind of joyous verse he had composed while living in Wales. And above all, he felt that as a person he still remained a stranger in a strange land, an outsider. Thus, he questioned the *fairness* or rather the "justice" of his Lord. (*Justice* is to me such a cold word. I would never pray to God for justice, for no man or woman should chance a plea for justice; rather, one should pray for mercy.) We cannot condemn Hopkins for feeling so; we can only and *justifiably* feel compassion: he is so heartbreakingly human. One would have to be made of stone not to feel his pain.

One last comment on "Carrion Comfort": in the last line, even though Hopkins feels that his Lord has treated him unjustly, he still refers to him as "O thou lord of life." Although he feels abandoned, *he* does not abandon his Lord; such is the depth of his love. The lover still comes back no matter what the treatment. It should be mentioned that some critics see masochism in Hopkins' poetry, an observation I'm not prepared to comment on, for it would require a rereading of his entire opus. But it's something to keep in mind for future readings, for Hopkins' poetry is multilayered and fascinating, and one can always find something new on rereading his work, as one does with reading Shakespeare. I taught *King Lear* for twenty-five years and never tired of it because I always found new insight. Same with Hopkins...

Next is the gentlest of the Terrible Sonnets: "My own heart let me more have pity on; let / Me live to my sad self hereafter kind." Here we meet a man who realizes that he has been too hard on himself, that he's in dire need of his own pity: he must love and forgive himself. For what? For being Gerard Manley Hopkins. He has not been kind to his "sad self." He has not practiced Christ's teaching to love his neighbor as he loves himself. He hasn't loved himself; therefore, how can he fully love others? We may indeed ask if he has *ever* loved himself.

But his suffering isn't over. He's still tormented: "With this tormented mind tormenting yet." We again think of King Lear calling upon the gods not to let him go mad. Like the blind Gloucester, Hopkins staggers through his days "by groping round my comfortless" life.

He's still in the dark; his eyes blind "in their dark." He's not only blind and lost but he's also incapable of finding water to quench his thirst "in all a world of wet." We think of the Ancient Mariner who sees water everywhere but none to drink. Hopkins then addresses himself, as he does in the first line: "Soul, self; come poor Jackself." I think of poor Edgar of King Lear, who had to disguise himself as a Bedlam beggar to survive and who referred to himself as poor Tom: "Poor Turlygod! Poor Tom! / That's something yet. 'Edgar' I nothing am" (2.3.20—21).

Hopkins still feels he's a nothing, but out of pity for himself he begs himself to "call off thoughts awhile / Elsewhere; leave comfort root-room." Whereas before he calls upon his Lord to send his roots rain, now he calls upon himself to leave him some space: he feels confined like a prisoner in a small, darkened cell.

His courage isn't as visible as that of Edgar, who will "outface" all that is out to destroy him, but it's there obscured by darkness. Hopkins hasn't given up, and he'll allow joy to "size / At God knows when to God knows what." Here there is a Christian surrender to God's will—not my will but yours be done. This is the positive interpretation, but the other is that Hopkins will no longer exists; he must surrender it and hope for revivifying beauty, to see again sunlight "betweenpie mountains—lights a lovely mile."

Whereas Edgar is proactive in his own survival, Hopkins is passive, yet he is still in the game, still alert, and a part of him knows that the adversary is not so much "out there" but inside him; it's the reason he summons pity to be bestowed on his "poor Jackself." If he can elicit this pity, he will be offered a "lovely mile," enough distance perhaps to get him through his darkness.

I'm now approaching the end of my walk with Hopkins, but I don't wish to conclude on a sad note, not on one of the Terrible Sonnets. I'll end positively with one of his happy lyrics composed when he was studying at St. Beuno's in Wales.

Today we know enough about psychology to understand the utmost importance of recognizing the needs of our own particular temperament and personality. If a person is quiet, shy, or introverted, such a one must live a life that corresponds to what he or she is. This will apply not only to lifestyle but also to the choice of employment.

Hopkins was never meant to work in poverty-stricken urban parishes. He was too high-strung to teach youngsters, who would have taken advantage of his gentle, kindhearted nature. If we closely investigate his life, we discover that he was most happy at Oxford and St. Beuno's College. He was an academic, and he should've been allowed to remain in academia, but because he favored Duns Scotus' theology over that of Thomas Aquinas, his academic career as a Jesuit lecturer was doomed.

But while studying theology at St. Beuno's, he was happy, and likely for several reasons. Above all, St. Beuno's was located in one of the most beautiful locations of Wales, and Hopkins was always drawn to nature's beauty. The order and structure of life at the college was also an important factor in his happy psychological state. And as I've mentioned so many times, he wrote his best poetry at St. Beuno's. Thus, I would like to end my book with a poem he composed there: "As kingfishers catch fire, dragonflies draw flame."

Poets and birds just go together. It's not so mysterious that they would, for birds can fly, and every poet hopes to fly with inspiration. Many birds are exquisitely beautiful, as is the kingfisher. It's beautiful of itself—that's its God-given characteristic—but when the sun flashes upon it, it brings out even more the beauty of its azure feathers and its sometimes-red breast. Each kingfisher is a one of a kind, one of God's masterpieces, as is the dragonfly, a smaller creature of flight, but it too shines to a flame when drenched in sunlight.

With the lines "As tumbled over in roundy wells / Stones ring, like each tucked string tells," Hopkins is recalling his game of dropping stones into a well. Each stone has its own individual sound as it hits the water's surface, like the "tucked" or plucked sound of a violin or harp. No plucked string ever records exactly the same note, just as every snowflake is different from every other snowflake.

Hopkins loved the bells of Oxford, where there are many that announce the hours. And the bells of Oxford are so individual that each has its own name. In describing how "each hung bell's / Bow swung finds tongue to fling out broad its name," Hopkins reminds us that the clapper, the "tongue" of each bell, creates its own individual sound, its own "name." No bell sounds alike. Much goes into the sound of a bell, depending on how big it is and the weight of its metal, that of the clapper and that of its rounded bell-shape, especially the thickness of the bell's rim.

Just as birds, dragonflies, and bells glorify their Creator, so do mortals when they do the thing that they were born to do. Hopkins believed, as did Scotus, in the *haecceitas* or thisness of each thing and of each human being: each person is one of a kind, and only he or she can be that person. Hopkins was intrigued by Scotus' way of looking at the world because it emphasizes the world's variety and diversity. It also glorifies God's infinity, for everything, when closely observed, offers us a glimpse of divinity. Thus Hopkins can state, "Each mortal thing does one thing and the same: / Deals out that being indoors each one dwells."

Within each of us is that individual divine spark, peculiar to only that person. No one is like any other human being. Each of us is unique and made in the image of God, and of God there is only infinite variety, a boundless treasure of characteristics and gifts.

Just as we cannot fall out of the universe, we cannot fall out of ourselves: Hopkins is "myself." His self spells his name: Gerard Manley Hopkins. No one can escape his or her self: each creature "selves—goes itself; *myself* it speaks and spells; / Crying *Whát I dó is me: for that I came.*" Each thing that exists speaks itself (note Hopkins' use of the colloquial "*goes* itself") as if speaking a word, just as when God spoke himself, the word he spoke was Christ, God among us. The glory of selfhood is God's gift to each of us.

So many people question the meaning of life. The existentialists say it's the ultimate question. Hopkins offers the answer: the meaning of life is to be you. You came into the world to be you and to do the things only you can do. We hear an echo of Shakespeare's maxim: "To thine own self be true." Yes, if we are true to ourselves, then we are true to life and to God.

To conclude the poem, Hopkins turns from creation in general, and even from humanity in general, to focus on the "just man," by which he mean the "human person fully alive" (to quote St. Irenaeus of Lyons), the adjusted person, the man or woman who is right with the world and with God and thus "acts in God's eye what in God's eye he is." Such persons become to the world around them a sacrament, an image of "Christ. For Christ plays in ten thousand places, /

Lovely in limbs, and lovely in eyes not his / To the Father through the features of men's faces."

This poem wouldn't exist had not Hopkins discovered Scotus and his concept of *haecceitas*. Thus, this poem could be interpreted as a thank-you from Hopkins to Scotus. It should also be noted that this poem wasn't shared with anyone, not even with Robert Bridges. It was found among Hopkins' papers after his death. There is only one sheet with many corrections, and scholars are able by comparing the handwriting to date it to his time at St. Beuno's.

Dear Father Hopkins,

I discovered your poetry in my Catholic high school, and I was very moved by your delight in the beauty of the world. Some of your poems I found difficult to understand, but I returned to your verse when I became a young adult majoring in English literature at college. Your brilliance and poetic innovations won me for life.

I knew that in your lifetime you had a reading audience of two: Canon Dixon and your best friend, Robert Bridges. Bridges could sometimes be rather harsh in his criticism of your verse, but on some level he must have recognized your genius for he saved every poem you ever sent to him. It was he who finally introduced you to the world. What a boon for poetry lovers everywhere!

As a teacher of English literature, I loved teaching your lyrics, most of them composed when you were studying theology at St. Beuno's in Wales. The beauty of Wales was obviously your muse, inspiring you to compose some of your best poems, ones that have become famous throughout the English-speaking world. When I taught your verse, however, I steered clear of your masterpiece, *The*

Wreck of the Deutschland, because it's too difficult for high school students, even the gifted ones I taught. It was even difficult for your dear friend Bridges, who called it a dragon of a poem. Its multi-meanings reveal themselves only after many close readings of the text.

As I grew older, I found myself intrigued by your Dublin poems, those that are known as the "Terrible Sonnets." Nowhere in the poetry I've read have I met such pain and anguish as appears in these poems. To be frank, I was astonished that you were so depressed that you, a supposedly happy priest, considered suicide. I wanted to know why; thus, I began to read everything I could about you. I read all the biographies, some of which were very helpful, but in the end I realized I had to return to your poetry, for it truly is your autobiography.

I now know you suffered from depression, and it is perhaps one of the reasons I was attracted to your late verse, for I too have suffered from depression for much of my life. Your poems reveal a soul tossed and battered by depression, but they are also a testament to your endurance, to your survival. I'm convinced that you likely survived because you possessed an outlet in composing poetry, that and your belief in and love of Christ.

So here I am, a person of the twenty-first century turning to a man of the nineteenth century for hope and inspiration. You have indeed offered me both through your verse, but also through your journals, sermons, and letters. And for that I simply want to say thank-you.

And by the way, the fame you yearned for so much in your life, well, it came true. You are one of the most famous poets in the world, beloved wherever English is read, and you have been translated into many languages. Worldwide fame—it is what I would describe as a triumph.

Sincerely yours,

Robert Waldron

Notes

Introduction

1. Brother Patrick Hart, OCSO, *The Literary Essays of Thomas Merton* (New York: A New Directions Book, 1981), 346.

2. Gerard Manley Hopkins, *Poetry and Prose*, ed. Walford Davies (New York: Alfred A. Knopf, 1995), 161.

3. Ibid., 218—19.

First Reading of Gerard Manley Hopkins

1. Ralph Harper, *On Presence: Variations and Reflections* (Philadelphia: Trinity Press International, 1991), 77.

2. Ibid.

3. C. C. Abbot, ed., *Further Letters of Gerard Manley Hopkins, Including His Correspondence with Coventry Patmore* (London: Oxford University Press, 1938), 213.

4. Ibid., 109—10.

5. William Styron, *Darkness Visible: A Memoir of Madness* (New York: Random House, 1990), 36—37.

6. Evelyn Underhill, *The Mystic Way: A Psychological Study in Christian Origins* (London: J. M. Dent & Sons, LTD, 1913), 55.

7. R. F. Clark, "The Training of a Jesuit," *Nineteenth Century* xl (August 1896), 211—25.

8. Interview in *The Brooklyn Rail*, October 2008. Poets Sally Dawidoff and Jean Gallagher visited Marie Ponsot's Upper East Side apartment just before she handed in her sixth collection of poetry—a

yet-untitled manuscript—to Knopf. Accessible at http://www.brooklynrail.org/2008/10/books/marie-ponsot-with-sally-dawidoff-and-jean-gallagher

Conversion

1. James Joyce, *A Portrait of an Artist as a Young Man* (New York: Penguin Group, 1991), 128.

2. Adam Kirsch, "Back to Basics: How Gerard Manley Hopkins Remade English Poetry," *New Yorker* (May 11, 2009): 106—7.

3. C. C. Abbot, ed., *Further Letters of Gerard Manley Hopkins, Including His Correspondence with Coventry Patmore*, 2nd edition (London: Oxford University Press, 1970), 213.

4. Richard William Church, *The Oxford Movement* (London: Oxford University Press, 1891), 18.

5. Abbot, *Further Letters*, 116—17.

6. Martin Cohen, *The Poems and Letters of Digby Mackworth Dolben, 1848—1867* (Atlantic Highlands, NJ: Humanities Press, 1981), 171.

7. C. C. Abbot, ed., *The Letters of Gerard Manley Hopkins to Robert Bridges* (London: Oxford University Press, 1970), 16—17.

8. John Henry Newman, *Apologia Pro Vita Sua* (London: Oxford University Press, 1913), v.

9. Humphrey House, ed., *The Journals and Papers of Gerard Manley Hopkins* (London: Oxford University Press 1959), 358.

10. Ibid., 146.

11. Abbot, *Further Letters*, 26.

12. Ibid.

13. C. S. Dessain and Thomas Gornall, eds., *Letters and Diaries of John Henry Newman* (Edinburgh: Thomas Nelson and Sons, 1961), n. p.

14. McNichols' poem was in a small brochure of his poetry printed in 2007, titled *Fire Above, Water Below: Poetry for the Spiritual Children of St. Francis and St. Clare.* No other information is available.

15. Jay Parini, *Why Poetry Matters* (New Haven, CT: Yale University Press, 2008), ix.

16. Sian Miles, ed., *Simone Weil: An Anthology* (New York: Grove Press), 212.

17. Robert Bernard Martin, *Gerard Manley Hopkins: A Very Private Life* (New York: G. P. Putnam's Sons, 1991), 203.

18. Sandra M. Gilbert, *Acts of Attention: The Poems of D. H. Lawrence* (Carbondale and Edwardsville: Southern Illinois University Press, 1990), 6.

19. Martin, *Gerard Manley Hopkins*, 223.

Years at St. Beuno's

1. Naomi Margolis Maurer, *The Pursuit of Spiritual Wisdom: The Thought and Art of Vincent van Gogh and Paul Gauguin* (London: Associated University Presses Inc., 1999), 74.

2. Paddy Kitchen, *Gerard Manley Hopkins: A Biography* (New York: Atheneum, 1979), 181.

3. Mary Oliver, *New and Selected Poems*, vol. 1 (Boston: Beacon Press, 1992), 10.

4. Mary Oliver, *White Pine* (New York: Harcourt, Brace, 1994), 8.

5. Dennis O'Driscoll, *Stepping Stones: Interviews with Seamus Heaney* (New York: Farrar, Straus and Giroux, 2008), 36.

6. Ibid., 38.

7. Jay Parini, *Why Poetry Matters* (New Haven, CT: Yale University Press, 2008), 179.

8. John L. Mahoney, ed., *Seeing into the Life of Things: Essays on Religion and Literature* (New York: Fordham University Press, 1998), 220—21.

9. Parini, *Why Poetry Matters*, 17.

10. Adam Kirsch, "Back to Basics: How Gerard Manley Hopkins Remade English Poetry," *The New Yorker* (May 11, 2009), 106.

11. George Santayana, *Soliloquies in England* (New York: Charles Scribner's Sons, 1924), 109.

12. H. Emerson Fosdick, *Riverside Sermons* (New York: Harper Brothers, 1958), 8.

The Dublin Years

1. Paul Mariani, *Gerard Manley Hopkins: A Life* (New York: Viking, 2008), 295.

2. Ibid.

3. C. C. Abbot, ed., *Letters of Gerard Manley Hopkins to Robert Bridges* (Oxford: Oxford University Press), 191.

4. Ibid.

5. Ibid., 193.

6. Ibid., 216.

7. Ibid., 219.

8. Ibid.

9. Ibid., n. p.

10. Robert Bernard Smith, *Gerard Manley Hopkins: A Very Private Life* (New York: G. P. Putnam's Sons, 1991), 375.

11. Walt Whitman, *Leaves of Grass* (New York: Barnes and Noble Books, 1993), 33.

12. Thomas Merton, *Mystics and Zen Masters* (New York: Dell Publishing Co., 1961), 141.

13. T. S. Eliot, *The Complete Poems and Plays* (New York: Harcourt Brace Jovanovich, Publishers, 1950), 145.

14. Gwendolen Greene, ed., *Letters from Baron Friedrich von Hügel to a Niece* (London: J. M. Dent & Sons LTD, 1928), 166.

15. William Styron, *Darkness Visible: A Memoir of Madness* (New York: Vintage Books, 1990), 56.

16. Paul Mariani, *Commentary on the Complete Poems of Gerard Manley Hopkins* (Ithaca, NY: Cornell University Press), 224.

Bibliography

Abbot, C. C., ed. *The Letters of Gerard Manley Hopkins to Robert Bridges.* London: Oxford University Press, 1955.

————. *The Further Letters of Gerard Manley Hopkins, Including His Correspondence with Coventry Patmore.* London: Oxford University Press, 1956.

Davies, Walford. *Gerard Manley Hopkins: Poetry and Prose.* London: J. M. Dent, 1998.

Gardner, W. H., and N. H. Mackenzie, eds. *The Poems of Gerard Manley Hopkins.* London: Oxford University Press, 1967.

House, Humphrey, ed. *The Journals and Papers of Gerard Manley Hopkins,* 2nd ed. London: Oxford University Press, 1966.

Ellsberg, Margaret R. *Created to Praise: The Language of Gerard Manley Hopkins.* New York: Oxford University Press, 1987.

Fosdick, Harry Emerson. *The Living of These Days.* New York: Harpers and Brothers, 1956.

Kitchen, Paddy. *Gerard Manley Hopkins: A Biography.* New York: Atheneum, 1979.

Lightman, Maria. *The Contemplative Poetry of Gerard Manley Hopkins.* Princeton, NJ: Princeton University Press, 1989.

Mariani, Paul. *Gerard Manley Hopkins: A Life.* New York: Viking, 2008.

Martin, Robert Bernard. *Gerard Manley Hopkins: A Very Private Life.* New York: G. P. Putnam's Sons, 1991.

Milward, Peter, SJ. *A Commentary on the Sonnets of G. M. Hopkins.* Chicago: Loyola University, 1969.

————. *A Lifetime with Hopkins.* Naples, FL: Sapientia Press, 2005.

Nichols, Aidan, OP. *Hopkins, Theologian's Poet.* Naples, FL: Sapientia Classics, 2006.

White, Norman. *Hopkins, A Literary Biography.* Oxford: Clarendon Press, 1992.